CONFESSION

CONFESSION

The Healing of the Soul

Peter Tyler

B L O O M S B U R Y
LONDON · OXFORD · NEW YORK · NEW DELHI · SYDNEY

Bloomsbury Continuum
An imprint of Bloomsbury Publishing Plc

50 Bedford Square
London
WC1B 3DP
UK

1385 Broadway
New York
NY 10018
USA

www.bloomsbury.com

Bloomsbury, Continuum and the Diana logo are trademarks of Bloomsbury
Publishing Plc

First published 2017

ISBN   TPB: 978-1-4729-3432-1
        EPDF: 978-1-4729-3430-7
        EPUB: 978-1-4729-3433-8

2 4 6 8 10 9 7 5 3 1

Typeset by Integra Software Services Pvt. Ltd.
Printed and bound in Great Britain by CPI Group (UK) Ltd, Croydon CR0 4YY

MIX
Paper from
responsible sources
FSC   FSC® C020471
www.fsc.org

To find out more about our authors and books visit www.bloomsbury.com. Here you
will find extracts, author interviews, details of forthcoming events and the option to
sign up for our newsletters.

CONTENTS

INTRODUCTION

WHY CONFESSION?

Inside the huge Romanesque church the tourists jostled in the half darkness.
Vault gaped behind vault, no complete view.
A few candle-flames flickered.
An angel with no face embraced me
and whispered through my whole body:
'Don't be ashamed of being human, be proud!
Inside you vault opens behind vault endlessly.
You will never be complete, that's how it's meant to be.'
Blind with tears
I was pushed out on the sun-seething piazza
together with Mr and Mrs Jones, Mr Tanaka and Signora Sabatini
and inside them all vault opened behind vault endlessly.

Tomas Tranströmer, *Romanesque Arches*[1]

'Your heart condemns you. But God is greater than your heart and knows all things.'[2]

We are strangers to ourselves.

This fundamental insight lies at the heart of this book and, as the poet suggests, at the heart of human life. Various traditions have arisen to seek solutions to this problem. However, the one that will concern us here is the practice of confession.

Within its traditional homeland, the Catholic Church, confession has become the 'Cinderella sacrament': the statistics and anecdotage suggest fewer and fewer people availing themselves of the sacrament, despite the best efforts of Pope Francis to bolster attendance. In the growing ranks of evangelicals and other reformed Christians it holds no significant sway, and within Orthodoxy it never possessed the central status that it possessed within the Western church. However, in the secular world, there has never been greater interest in the subject. The online *Oprah* magazine, for example, has a section devoted to 'confessing your deep, dark secrets'. As it states there:

> We all have a deep psychological need to be accepted as we really are, but that can never happen as long as there are parts of us that no one sees or knows. We conceal aspects of ourselves that we think invite rejection, but ironically, the very act of secrecy makes us inaccessible to love. We think we're hiding our secrets, but really, our secrets are hiding us.[3]

As well as seeing people for psychotherapy and spiritual direction, I regularly give talks at retreat houses and conferences and to those involved in pastoral care: clergy and laity alike. In these situations I often ask the questions: 'Why do people come to you?' 'Why are they seeking counselling, therapy or spiritual direction?' 'What are they after?'

The answer is clear: invariably they are not happy with themselves – they have an unhappy marriage, they don't like their work, they don't like their parish priest, they don't like their religious superior, they don't like their boss/husband/wife/mother/father/neighbourhood (delete as appropriate). For so many of us the simple fact is that we do not love ourselves, we are not at ease with ourselves and it is from this dis-ease, I will argue here, that the urge for confession arises. As we shall see in this book, our 'case-studies' – various men and women from different epochs and periods of history – have felt this 'dis-ease' and the desire to do something about it.

One of the key arguments of this book will be that confession is the first step towards learning to know ourselves. Of course, there are many types of false confession – the desire to have a 'clean slate' driven by self-hatred, guilt and blame, for example. We shall have to investigate these elements too. Yet, the main thrust of this book will be that confession arises from the desire for compassion not only to ourselves but to those around us.

Once we can experience self-forgiveness it is a lot easier to forgive others. We realize that things have to change in our lives, and often the first step in that change is the art of confession. I say 'art' because the practice and process of confession is an art. The therapist knows it, as do the pastoral worker and the priest. But what is that art, and how does the practice of confession take place?

To explore these questions I have written this book – primarily to explore the dynamics of confession and to set it against its long and rich history. As in my earlier books, I do not propose a comprehensive history of confession (if such a thing were possible, which I doubt) but, adopting a phrase from Michel Foucault and Friedrich Nietzsche, suggest a 'genealogy' of confession using selected key figures to map wider trends and tendencies that have shaped not only our understanding of confession but the *psyche*-soul in general.[4]

During the course of writing this book it became apparent to me that when we talk of confession we are describing at least two different movements within the human soul. On the one hand there is the wider human desire to bring balm to a wounded *psyche* as suggested above. As Berggren put it: 'it is common knowledge that talking about painful and disturbing memories or experiences which have lain on our minds unburdens us of them and affords a sense of relief'.[5] This, as we shall see, was central to the discoveries of the founding fathers of psychoanalysis, Sigmund Freud and Carl Jung. Indeed, a common argument that we shall explore in this book is that with the decline in religious practice in the later modern period, the psychoanalyst (or even the cab driver or hairdresser) has taken over the role of the Church in being the guardian of confession. Slipped from its metaphysical moorings, the ship of confession has certainly entered into new and unexpected waters in our contemporary world of psychological examination of motivation.

Yet, as I will argue here, to concentrate on the psychological dimension of confession is to tell only half its story. This, sadly, has often been the option of contemporary commentators. Taylor, for example, states that 'presented with options such a psychotherapy, few subjects would feel compelled to return to the Catholic Church to fulfil their confessional desires'.[6] Cornwell (2014) sees confession largely as a means to bring about deformation of character. While acknowledging the psychological value of confession (which will explain the present interest in the subject beyond the confines of the Church), this volume will also suggest that confession has a second, and equally important, role to play in the human person: to open a door in the *psyche* to the possibility of the transcendent.

With this insight in mind it thus becomes possible to trace two parallel 'genealogies' in the evolution of confession: on the one hand, the psychological desire for release from the suffering of existential anxiety, and on the other, the use of the apparatus of confession as a pursuit for the transcendent. These two aims, as we shall see, will sometimes coincide but at other times will conflict with each other, and in the second part of the book I shall trace some of these conflicts and a possible resolution.

In 2015 I completed the first part of what I hoped might be a trilogy of books concerning the contemporary relationship between psychology and spirituality. This first part, *The Pursuit of the Soul*, was essentially a prolegomenon for the other parts of the series, of which this is the second. In it I investigated the origins of both Christianity and contemporary psychoanalysis by asking fundamental questions about the nature of the soul-*psyche* in both traditions. The result of this research somewhat surprised me in that I found the answers to the questions I was posing in the final works of the great twentieth-century Jewish-Christian martyr Edith Stein (St Teresa Benedicta a Cruce), who died in Auschwitz in 1942. Stein, drawing heavily on St Augustine, among others, defined the human person as that which looks simultaneously both at the worldly and at the transcendent in the same gaze. The same gaze, in fact, which she imputed to Jesus Christ, the God-man.

Whereas that first book was more concerned with the nature or metaphysics of the self as seen through the eyes of Christianity and psychoanalysis, this second book will concentrate on the 'healing of the soul' through the dynamic *praxis* of confession. I concluded the earlier book by suggesting that we approach discourse about the soul with a certain care. Because of its gossamer-fine nature, the intellect will often have to take a back seat as we observe the movements of the soul by means of paradox, symbol, myth, the relational and the libidinal.

Within the present book, this practice is adopted. So, as well as providing a theological, philosophical and historical exegesis of the nature of confession, I shall discuss the soul from the mythological and symbolic perspective. Indeed, it is noticeable how many of the individual confessors we shall examine often move beyond the coolly logical to the symbolic and libidinal in their struggle to express themselves. This holds true for one of my confessional 'case-studies', the Austrian philosopher Ludwig Wittgenstein (1889–1951). An inveterate confessor, Wittgenstein's thought demonstrates how the practice of 'saying and showing' reveals the essence of human communication. Rather than a distraction, confession for Wittgenstein becomes the essence of what it is to be a human being. From his 'philosophical confessions' we shall see a door opens on to the transcendent through the practice of confession.

In contrast to my earlier work, I will look to the East and the contemporary struggle to determine how differing religious cultures may interact. Consequently, my second 'postmodern' confessor will be the French priest Henri Le Saux (1910–73), who, after the end of the Second World War, travelled to India to find a synthesis between the East and the West. While there, he mapped the journey of his soul by exploring his innermost experiences in a confessional diary. Like Wittgenstein before him, Swami Abhishiktananda, as he came to be known, sought to reconcile the psychological demands of absolute honesty with his own search for the transcendent, with unexpected consequences.

In the confessions of both Wittgenstein and Le Saux we reach the edges of human discourse, and both, as we shall see, move ultimately into silence and poetry. As this volume begins with a poem, so it will be in the confessional poetry of St John of the Cross that it will end. St John offers a reconciliation between the psychological and transcendent dimensions of confession for, in his writings, we encounter a contemporary who struggles with the universal theme of identity and transcendence in the search for truth.

Most of the writing of this book took place during the tumultuous events of 2016, which began as a summer storm in the United Kingdom in the June referendum and then swept first across the Atlantic and then on to mainland Europe. For those of us involved in these events, we found the securities and familiarities of fifty years disappear overnight. At the time of writing we are still in the process of reconstructing our polity and society. However, it seems, as with other such epic years as 1989, 1789 and even 1517, we are watching one world dying and a new one arising. This has informed my writing as I notice that at such times of instability there is a heightened need for discernment of spirit, purpose and action. My choice of conversation partners for this book – a North African, a Romanian, an Austrian, a Moravian, a Breton, a Swiss national, a Spaniard and a Celt (aided and assisted by Frenchmen, Russians and Danes) – reasserts my deeply held belief in the great Continental European humanistic and intellectual tradition which, at its best (as we see in many of the figures discussed here), can reach out to all places and all times in a universal dialogue of the spirit. In these uneasy times it seems wise for us all to examine our consciences and motives, to confess our faults, to allow the tortured twenty-first-century soul to begin the process of healing it so badly needs.

CHAPTER ONE

THE CONFESSING ANIMAL

In the introduction I asked why it might be the case today that confession in a secular sense has grown while interest in its traditional religious homelands has declined. A frequently cited answer to this conundrum is that the practice and rituals of the psychoanalyst's couch or counsellor's consulting room have replaced the iron grille of the confessional. This is an attractive proposal. From the time of Sigmund Freud and Carl Jung onwards, psychology, as we shall see, has always recognized its debt to its older sacramental brothers and sisters. In one of his first books, *Studies in Hysteria*, Freud acknowledged that the power of his nascent discipline lay in its ability to alleviate the 'strangulated effect' of the neurosis by helping it to find 'a way out through speech'.[1] Thus, the 'talking cure' was born. In the later *Question of Lay Analysis* (1925/6) he went further in suggesting that the therapist as 'secular father confessor' asks his patients not only to confess 'what they know and conceal from other people' but to go further – to confess what 'he does not know', too.[2] Likewise, Carl Jung in his 1929 essay, 'Die Probleme der modernen Psychotherapie',[3] admitted that confession was one of the pivotal mainstays of his own form of 'analytical psychology': 'the first beginnings of all analytical treatment are to be found in its prototype, the confessional'.[4] For, he continued, 'as soon as man was capable of conceiving the idea of sin, he had recourse to psychic concealment – or, to put it in analytical language, repressions arose. Anything that is concealed is a secret. The maintenance of secrets acts like a psychic poison which alienates their possessor from the community'.[5] Secrets, sin, guilt, repression and forgiveness – in such language the apparatus of psychoanalysis sought to appropriate the age-old traditions for its new modern ends. Yet it has not been simply the analysts who have been fascinated by the human choreography of confession. The French post-structuralist commentator Michel Foucault has gone so far as to call man 'the confessing animal'[6] – for him the practice lies at the heart of our human identity. He began his great three-volume discourse on the *History of Sexuality* with a lengthy exploration of the role of confession in establishing the legitimation of desire through discourse and the part this plays in the establishment by Freud and his followers of the present-day medicalized tradition of confession embodied and made manifest in the psychoanalyst's couch. Indeed, he goes further by suggesting that 'we have become a singularly confessing society':

> The confession has spread its effects far and wide. It plays a part in justice, medicine, education, family relationships, and love relations, in the most ordinary affairs of everyday life, and in the most solemn rites; one confesses one's crimes, one's sins, one's thoughts and desires, one's illnesses and troubles; one goes about telling, with the greatest precision, whatever is most difficult to tell.[7]

From these opening remarks, then, we can see that
confession is a double-headed beast – both secular panacea
and religious sacramental necessity. On the religious side,
starting from the Scriptures, we find numerous accounts of
the need to 'make a clean breast' and to 'repent' (the opening words of Mark's Gospel) among the early Christians.
As the small cult moved into the desert, the need for a
specific process of manifestation of conscience to another
was expressed for the early Christians in the teachings of
the desert fathers and mothers. Confession thus became
understood as a key 'spiritual exercise' of those seeking the
transcendent. This transcendent search through confession
(as we shall see in the next chapter) only became codified by
the Western church in its second millennium and indeed,
as we have seen, even this never happened in many parts of
Christianity. Thus, from the thirteenth century onwards its
evolution in the West became bound up with its identification as one of the sacraments of the Church whose practice
was inculcated on all good upstanding Christians.

However, the aim of this book is not simply to examine the phenomenon of confession from a theological or
sacramental perspective, but, in recognition of its double-
headed nature, it is also to explore it from what can be
termed a psycho-spiritual perspective. For as well as
acknowledging the role of the practice in the search for
the transcendent, we must also recognize its adoption in a
more secular context in its present-day manifestations in
'interrogations, consultations, autobiographical narratives
and letters'.[8] For, as Foucault points out, the apparatus of
confession – its great pantechnicon – has found its way
into all branches of contemporary society. Thus, as well

as tracing its religious and ecclesiastical roots, we need to examine how this 'psycho-spiritual' phenomenon has been able to bridge the gap that developed between the sacred and the secular in our current age. This will lead, in the present volume, to reflections on the psychological importance of confession and how much this has to bear on its present and future role in psycho-spiritual development. In doing this, as in so much of my recent work, I aim carefully to walk the tightrope between the Scylla of transcendental piety and the Charybdis of psychological reductionism. My contention and argument here is that we can only really understand the richness of this double-headed beast if we acknowledge not only its psychological verisimilitude but also its transcendent dimension.

In the following chapter I shall take the figure of the wounded Lord Tristan, cast adrift on his small skiff in the Irish Sea, as a symbol for the lost contemporary Western soul. Consequently, the analysis of this book, in accord with its subtitle, shall be an attempt to suggest a method of healing for that lost soul by means of confession. In arguing this I shall, in this and the following chapter, examine the origins of what I will call the transcendental wound of the contemporary soul before turning, in the final three chapters, to specific confessional experiences of three key Western figures: Ludwig Wittgenstein, Henri Le Saux and John of the Cross. By examining their confessions I will conclude that confession prescribes a means towards the healing of the soul in all its theological and psychological dimensions. I shall accordingly begin this process by examining the roots of the Christian confessional in the Scriptures and the early Christian practitioners of the art.

REPENT YE!

Jesus begins his earthly ministry with a call to repentance – 'μετανοεῖτε'[9] – for his 'kingdom' (*basileia*) is close at hand and the time (*kairos*) is upon us. This striking opening chord to Mark's Gospel persists throughout the Gospels as he repeats the call to repentance / *metanoia* as a constant theme in his teaching.[10] The Greek term is a compound from *meta* – 'after', 'with', 'beyond' – and *nous*, the mind, spirit or soul.[11] Thus Jesus demands that this following of him will require a change of attitude and mentality. In its Greek origins the term carries the notion of changing the mind, or coming to a new opinion, along with the notion of regret and remorse.[12] The Septuagint employs the term 14 times where it repeats the Greek notions of regret and changing of mind, thus subtly shifting understanding of sin and repentance inherited from the Jewish Scriptures.[13]

In the Jewish Scriptures commentators have noted a traditional emphasis on the group or social aspect of repentance. In books such as Joel,[14] Hosea[15] and Jonah,[16] the people of Israel take on group fasting, mourning and wearing of sackcloth and ashes in order to avert the wrath of Yahweh and re-establish the bond of covenant with the Almighty: 'put on sackcloth and lament, you priests; wail, you ministers of the altar. Come, pass the night in sackcloth, you ministers of my God! … Sanctify a fast, call a solemn assembly. Gather the elders and all the inhabitants of the land to the house of the Lord your God, and cry out to the Lord.'[17] As in this passage from the book of Joel, the general call for repentance has a cultic element where the priests will enact certain prescribed rites for the purposes of setting aright the relationship of the people of Israel with their God. However, within the Jewish scriptures other voices are heard: the prophets correct this emphasis on the public and exoteric expression of regret and draw back the people to God through the often-repeated phrase: 'return, come back to the Lord'. As Isaiah insists:

Is not this the fast that I choose: to loose the bonds of injustice, to undo the thongs of the yoke, to let the oppressed go free, and to break every yoke? Is it not to share your bread with the hungry, and bring the home-less poor into your house; when you see the naked, to cover them, and not to hide yourself from your kin? Then your light shall break forth like the dawn and your healing shall spring up quickly.[18]

As well as the public show of mourning and fasting the prophets insist that the people of Israel also 'turn again' to the Lord so that they 'rend their hearts' and not their clothing.[19] Thus the notion of conversion of heart and mind is deeply embedded in the traditions to which early Christianity was heir – a dual tradition that emphasized public acts of mourning and repentance as well as the more subtle personal 'conversion of heart'. As we shall see throughout this book, these two sides of confession will interact with each other throughout its long and fascinat-ing history.

In these early traditions we begin to see some of the key features of confession as it will develop in the West: an 'interior act' of conversion of will or attitude accom-panied by a concomitant external or ritualistic act of public behaviour and repentance. It has its origins in notions of regret and remorse, including the notion of having gone against the transcendent order. This transgression must be corrected through right actions and duties, which will also usually involve changing one's behaviour and attitudes, especially towards those who are considered less well-off or wronged by previous actions (e.g. in Luke's account of the parable of Dives and Lazarus[20] where Father Abraham calls Dives' family to turn from their selfish feasting to cognizance of the suffering of those around them). By such means a healing process is initiated – the healing of the *nous* or soul.

CASSIAN AND THE DESERT FATHERS AND MOTHERS

From its beginnings, early Christianity places a premium on the use of *diakresis* or 'the discernment of spirits', which will be necessary to create that essential *metanoia* so central to its spiritual tradition. Time and again the early desert fathers and mothers exhort their followers to heed the advice of St Paul and to 'examine yourselves and test yourselves',[21] noticing in particular that an apparently good action, deed or thought may have a harmful purpose or end. As we shall see, this call for 'self-knowledge' will be a recurring theme throughout the Christian tradition of confession.

Thus, we find in the desert fathers and mothers a moral anthropology that exhorts us to redirect the passions away from the destructive and towards the constructive. However, they continually also remember the advice of the elders that this must not take place in too hard or harsh

an environment that breaks the individual through excessive penance. As St Anthony explains in a famous passage:

> A hunter in the desert saw Abba Anthony enjoying himself
> with the brethren and was shocked. Wanting to show him
> that it was necessary sometimes to meet the needs of
> the brethren, the old man said to him, 'Put an arrow in
> your bow and shoot it.' So he did. The old man then said,
> 'Shoot another,' and he did so. Then the old man said,
> 'Shoot yet again,' and the hunter replied, 'If I bend my
> bow so much I will break it.' Then the old man said to
> him, 'It is the same with the work of God. If we stretch
> the brethren beyond measure they will soon break.'[22]

John Cassian in his *Conferences*[23] quotes with approval an
old Greek saying, 'extremes meet', and continues 'for the
extreme of fasting comes to the same end as overeating
does, and excessive prolongation of a vigil is as detrimen-
tal to a monk as the torpor of heavy sleep is'. The fathers
and mothers wisely counsel that we must always examine our *motives* for everything we do, not least our pious
and penitential acts. These, they counsel, are not above
the action of the destructive and harmful forces within
ourselves. The aim of the desert fathers and mothers is not
to seek penance for penance's sake but to engage in *ascesis*
or 'training' to enable us to come closer to God. For them,
there is a clear distinction between this 'training' of desire
and suppression or repression of desire, a theme we shall
return to later. We could say that they engender a 'hermeneutic of suspicion' within the seeker – never trust
your motives but always examine them.

Recognizing the danger of self-deception, the desert elders realized the importance of having a guide or at least someone to whom we can open up our consciences and thoughts. Indeed, Cassian in the *Conferences* sees this disclosure of thoughts as the most important element of the monk's life. 'Not only all our actions,' he writes, 'but even all our thoughts should be offered to the inspection of the elders, so that, not trusting in one's own judgement, one may submit in every respect to their understanding.'[24] For, 'as soon as a wicked thought has been revealed it loses its power, and even before the judgement of discernment is exercised the loathsome serpent ... departs as a kind of laughing stock and object of dishonour'.[25] As Freud and the early psychologists were to rediscover at the beginning of the twentieth century, the act of telling a secret or desire can often kill its power over us. The art of confession in the desert tradition realized that the *act of speaking* holds its own power over the passions of the soul. In this way spiritual direction and confession become a choreography between what is said and what is unsaid as the power of the utterance of the word cannot be denied, and it is one of the main driving motivations behind the confessional urge – a key theme to which we shall return throughout this book.

To illustrate the importance of such disclosure of one's inmost thoughts to others, Cassian tells the story of Abba Serapion, whom he had come across during his travels in the deserts of North Africa and Asia Minor earlier in his life. The young Serapion, when living with the old Abba Theonas, having eaten the main meal of the day would often hide a biscuit under his cloak so that he could eat it later on in his own cell. One evening a group of seekers came to the old Abba to hear a conference on gluttony and disordered desire. So upset was Serapion by what he heard, and overcome with remorse, that he threw the biscuit on to the floor and begged mercy and indulgence from the old Abba for his theft. The kindly old man, however, said to the boy: 'Take heart, my boy. Your confession freed you from this captivity even before I spoke. Today you have triumphed over your conqueror and adversary, defeating him by your confession more decisively than you yourself had been overthrown by him because of your silence.'[26] No sooner had the Abba finished speaking than a sulphurous flame appeared from the young man's breast and left all in the room astonished as he wept for his sins.

Traditionally, then, the process of confession happened through two means, the disclosure of temptations and desires to another more experienced seeker, and the process of 'seeking a word' from a spiritual elder. Cassian is at pains to stress, however, that this discernment of spirits is not necessarily a gift of grey hairs and many years. The elderly are as much prone to deception as the young.[27] He gives numerous examples of this. One such was the elder Heron who, though revered by many disciples, finally took his own life, jumping down a well after a devil – 'disguised as an angel of light' – tricked him into thinking that God's angels would protect him as he jumped and that the miracle would bring many more to the faith. As Cassian states:

Just as all young men are not similarly fervent in spirit and instructed in discipline and the best habits, so neither in fact can all the elders be found to be similarly perfect and upright. For the riches of elders are not to be measured by their grey hairs but by the hard work of their youth and the deserts of their past labours.[28]

Once having carefully selected a guide, Cassian counsels suspicion of motives. True discernment of spirits requires a hermeneutic of suspicion regarding the very nature of ourselves. Within this tradition, then, *everything* we experience must be explored with another, nothing should be left out of our account of the seeker to her fellow Christians: 'Everything that is thought of is offered to the inspection of the elders, so that, not trusting one's own judgement, one may submit in every respect to their understanding and may know how to judge what is good and bad according to what they have handed down.'[29] This suspicion of motives goes alongside a deep humility in following the advice of the one to whom the seeker discloses their story. Just as a client seeking therapy today must trust the skill of the therapist and open themselves up to their judgement, so we find the same relationship in the desert tradition.

Part of the practice of this humility in the disclosure to the elder is for the penitent to free themselves from the tyranny of desire. Or from the subtle twists of the ego that identify ourselves with our own desires and 'projects'. This attachment Cassian calls a 'dragon's gall' and far worse than the drunkenness of wine or the gluttony of food.[30] We must be careful then to 'reject with unwavering strictness of mind those things which cater to our power and which have the appearance of a kind of goodness'.[31] Again, we are in the world of subtle self-delusion, made stronger by the apparent cloak of respectability which those who are involved in altruistic or religious works often wrap themselves up with, the more to bring delusion upon themselves and others. Evagrius of Pontus, another chronicler of the desert sayings, calls it the 'spirit of vainglory', and his pen portrait of its poison is psychologically subtle and still relevant today:

> The spirit of vainglory is most subtle and it readily grows up in the souls of those who practise virtue. It leads them to desire to make their struggles known publicly, to hunt after the praise of men. This in turn leads to their illusory healing of women, or to their hearing fancied sounds as the cries of demons ... It has men knocking at the door, seeking audiences with them. If the monk does not willingly yield to their request, he is bound and led away. When in this way he is carried aloft by vain hope, the demon vanishes and the monk is left to be tempted by the demon of pride or of sadness.[32]

The confessor, then, must be an astute counsellor and psychologist. However, over and above it all, the fathers counsel compassion towards those who struggle. Spiritual guides must never get too haughty and feel they are morally superior to those who come seeking confession. The weakness of the passions can strike anyone at any time. Cassian gives the telling story of the young man troubled with lust who goes to see the elder who scorns him and tells him he is not worthy of the life of a monk. As he leaves, dejected, to return to the fleshpots of a local town he meets another wiser elder, Abba Apollos. Unlike the first father, Apollos shows compassion and discloses that he himself has to struggle with this demon on a regular basis. As he prays for the young man the demons assail the first old man with the temptations. This old man now 'runs around hither and thither as if he were crazed and drunk',[33] finally setting off on the same route to the local fleshpots. In his 'obscene excitement' Abba Apollos confronts him, asking innocently where the former upright father is now heading. Realizing that he has been deceiving himself and others, the old man falls abashed at Apollos' feet. Apollos' final words to the would-be confessor are magnificent:

> The Lord let you be wounded by this so that at least in your old age you might learn to be compassionate toward others' infirmities and might be taught by your own example and experience to be considerate with respect to the frailty of the young ... Learn to be compassionate to those who struggle and never frighten with bleak despair those who are in trouble or unsettle them with harsh words. Instead encourage them mildly and gently.[34]

This tradition of compassion and gentleness has remained within the Christian practice of spiritual guidance and confession up to today.

Thus from the monastic and desert traditions the early church developed a model of confession that was non-liturgical and informational – more akin, in many respects, to our modern notion of counselling. Without a canonical formula the advice was given to help individual monks, and later lay-people, to find their way back to God through greater wisdom and discernment in their approach to their passions and desires.[35] As described by St John Climacus (c.579–c.649) in his *Ladder of Ascent*, confession, or *exomologisis* as he terms it, is something that may happen both within the liturgical context of the Church and beyond it. The spiritual father chosen by the monk need not necessarily be a priest (Climacus himself was probably not ordained),[36] the overriding metaphor being that the confessor is more like a doctor who heals with 'surgery, bandaging and cauterization'.[37] The patient (the penitent) bears the treatment with trust in the skill of the doctor. Such confession, in contrast to the Western Roman practice we shall discuss in the next chapter, can occur on a regular basis and in many respects, as we shall see later, has more in common with contemporary understandings of counselling than the Western notion of exculpation of sins at infrequent periods. For, as Metropolitan Kallistos Ware points out,[38] the monk confesses not only sins but also thoughts and *logismoi*, whether they are good, bad or neutral. Ware stresses that throughout, 'John (Climacus) employs by preference imagery that is therapeutic rather than juridical. Confession does not merely bestow absolution from guilt, understood in a formal or legalistic fashion, but on a deeper, more organic level it confers healing and restoration in wholeness. Sin is disease, to go to confession is to enter the hospital.'[39]

Having focused so far on the therapeutic role of confession among the desert elders, we turn now to the other aspect of confession in the early church that we need to explore: the theological perspective on confession given by, among others, St Augustine.

ST AUGUSTINE: FATHER OF CONFESSION?

Of all the early accounts of confession in the emerging Christian tradition, that of Augustine, the troubled saint of Hippo, North Africa, stands out in terms of its literary, cultural and theological influence.[40] Yet, as numerous commentators have pointed out, it is certainly not a straightforward confession in either the contemporary or classic use as explored above, but rather is a subtle and shifting literary and theological exegesis whose changing perspectives can often take the (usually unsuspecting) reader by surprise. In many respects it is the grand-daddy of the literary confession, a genre to which we shall return throughout the book. For, as Augustine repeatedly states, he wants to make a clean breast of things and present the confessional practice as the public saying of what had hitherto been concealed. However Augustine's sophisticated and complex character produces something much more interesting than a straightforward admission of guilt.

Augustine had been exposed to and had knowledge of most of the intellectual strands circulated in late antiquity, including neo-Platonism, Manichean dualism, Ciceronian rhetoric, Stoicism and his final beloved Christianity, centred on the teachings and writings of his mentor, St Ambrose of Milan.[41]

Accordingly, given this level of influence, we should not be surprised that 'the *Confessions*' is a complicated and subtle volume that works all these strands into a sophisticated confessional tapestry. To reduce the book to the misogynistic rantings of a deluded man (as some commentators would prefer) is effectively not to have read it. As Augustine writes in the book: 'I have become a great question to myself' (*factus eram ipse mihi magna quaestio*),[42] and this, if anything, is the driving dynamic behind this enormously influential book.

In one of his last works, the *Retractions*, Augustine says of the *Confessions*: 'the thirteen books of my *Confessions* praise the just and good God for my evil and good acts, and lift up the understanding and affection of men to Him. At least as far as I am concerned, they had this effect on me while I was writing them and they continue to have it when I am reading them.'[43] From this statement we can see two pointers as to the importance of Augustine's work. First, that the act of confession itself is a *performative* rather than an *informative* act. We shall return to this later. Second, as commentators such as O'Donnell point out, for Augustine the confessional act is bound up with praise and thanksgiving towards God as well as with the public disclosure of faults. Although, as we have seen, this second usage is found in its biblical context it is something not present in its classical Roman uses.[44]

Confession in its Roman pre-Christian usage had usually been associated with admitting the truth of a claim, normally in a legal trial. It was the *con-fateor* – the making known, owning up to and acknowledging of another's presence.[45] When transferred to emerging Christianity, the act of professing the truth was passed to the first Christian martyrs, who had been witnesses to the truth of their faith in Jesus Christ by execution and death. As McGinn points out, this Christian use was emphasized by the frequent use of the word *confiteor* in the Latin translations of the Scriptures, especially the Psalms (where it is found 65 times).[46] As Augustine puts it in the *Expositions of the Psalms*: 'Confession is twofold; it can be of sin or of praise. When things are going badly for us, in the midst of tribulations let us confess our sins; when things are going well for us, in our joy at his righteousness let us confess praise to God. Only let us never give up confession.'[47]

Thus, after Augustine, the old act of saying the truth through confession, the *confessio peccatorum* or confession of sins, is now increasingly linked with the *confessio laudis*, the act of praising God, and the *confessio fidei*, the profession of faith in the living Lord Jesus Christ.[48] As McGinn puts it: 'For Augustine *confessio* was not some secondary exercise of the soul converted to God; it was the foundation of the Christian life, what he called the "first thought" (*prima cogitatio*), so that he could even say, ". . . without confession we would not exist" (*sine confessione non simus*).'[49]

In a magisterial essay on Augustine's *Confessions*, McGinn sees the act of *confessio* as an essential element of what he terms the formation of the 'mystical self'. In this respect he defines the act of confession as 'a mental, oral or written act by which a person affirms God's truth, admits one's guilt, and thereby praises God's goodness'.[50] These three aspects of confession he designates as, first, the *confessio laudis*, 'the act of praise and thanksgiving for God's great gifts', with which the *Confessions* begins. Second, the *confessio peccati*, confession of sins, with which Augustine continues his account and which comprises a large proportion of the book. And finally the *confessio fidei*, or confession of faith, with which Augustine, now converted, concludes his book. Thus, for McGinn, confession 'is not just one of the speech-acts that humans use in addressing God; it is the formal feature of all speaking to God'.[51] In this last statement McGinn succinctly analyses the importance of Augustine's work to the subsequent history of confession. From this point onwards confession is not just *a* tool for the healing of the lost soul, but rather it is *the* means, par excellence, by which the soul, will be able to encounter the transcendent. In this respect the mode of confession goes not only to the heart of what it is to be a Christian but also to the heart of what it is to be a human being. For Augustine, argues McGinn, the means by which confession performs this role is through purification of the memory. 'Great is the power of memory', the bishop writes in Book Ten of the *Confessions*:

> A thing, O my God, to be in awe of, a profound and infinite multiplicity, and this is my soul, and this is whom I am (*et hoc animus est, et hoc ego ipse sum*). What then am I, O my God? What is my nature? A varied, multi-modal and immensely vehement life (*varia, multimoda vita et immense vehementer*). In the innumerable fields, dens and caverns of my memory, innumerably full of numberless kinds of things, either present by their images as are all bodies, or in themselves as our mental capacities, or by certain notions or awarenesses, like the affections of the soul – and I move swiftly from one to another and I penetrate them as deeply as I can, but find no end (*et finis nusquam*).[52]

Through the process of confession memory itself will be surpassed, for 'I shall climb beyond my power of memory, I shall mount beyond it, to come to You, O sweet light (*transibo eam ut pertendam ad te, dulce lumen*)'.[53] From this point onwards confession for the West will become not only a speech act among many but the means by which the individual mind is set on the path to the transcendent, the 'sweet light', wherein God dwells: 'I shall climb up beyond that power of mine called memory, longing to attain to touch You at the point where that contact is possible ... I shall pass beyond memory to find You. O truly good and certain loveliness (*vere bone, secura suavitas*).'[54] As we shall see in the next chapter, this notion will eventually be formalized in Christian consciousness by the agreement that confession is one of the seven sacraments of the Church – one of the special ways by which God mediates grace to His people.

Paraphrasing McGinn, confession thus becomes a 'mystical act' for it opens us up to the essential mystery that lies at the heart of our selves. If, as the book of Genesis says, we are made in the 'image and likeness of God', there must then be a profound unknowing that lies at the heart of the self. The confessional act, by initiating that conversation in the soul between the individual and the transcendent, must then be an act of unknowing, an act of mystery, that makes us 'strangers to ourselves'. As we move through our confessional accounts in the latter half of this book we shall see how one of the clear urges to confess is the desire to touch that element of unknowing that lies at the heart of the human self. For, as Augustine admits in Book Ten of the *Confessions*, only God can ultimately really know us and we can never truly know ourselves.

I will confess therefore what I know of myself and what I do not know (*confitear ergo quid de me sciam, confitear et quid de me nesciam*). For what I know of myself I know

through the shining of Your light and what I do not know
of myself I continue not to know until my darkness shall
be made as noonday in your countenance.[55]

After Augustine, confession will therefore become the
royal road to the transcendent as we have our confessional
conversation with God.

THE ROYAL ROAD TO GOD

According to Trapè, 'the essential task of Augustinian spirituality is the restoration of the image of God to man',[56]
or, as Augustine himself puts it in the *Literal Commentary
on Genesis*: 'It was in the very factor in which he surpasses
non-rational animate beings that man was made in God's
image. That, of course, is reason (*ratio*) itself, or *mens*
(mind) or *intelligentia* (intelligence) or whatever we wish
to call it.'[57] As Augustine develops his thought he elab-
orates the essential insight of the *Confessions* that we are
made 'in the image and likeness of God' and that by the
process of confession (in all its three forms) we can return
to that restored Godhead within. Thus when he writes
the second edition of his last, great masterpiece, *On the
Trinity*, between AD 413 and 420, he connects the 'image'
of the divine to the nature of the human soul – in particular with reference to memory, will and understanding.[58]
In this respect Augustine, in contrast to his contemporary
neo-Platonic seekers who had influenced him so much as a
young man, places Christ as the key mediator and educator
of the soul who will draw us into our Trinitarian identity.
Christ, for Augustine, is 'the way, the truth and the life'[59]

and, as he says in his *Homily on the Psalms* 84.1: 'The Lord himself heals the eyes of our hearts to enable us to see what he shows us.'[60]

Intimacy with the *persona Christi* will thus lead to the divinization of the soul, not through our own efforts or through merits of our own, but simply through the love and grace of God freely given: 'the Son of God was made a sharer in our mortal nature so that mortals might become sharers in his Godhead'[61] and 'It is quite obvious that God called human beings "gods" in the sense that they were deified by his grace, not because they were born of his own substance ... he alone deifies who is God of himself, not by participation in any other'.[62] Thus God deifies us only by adoption, through no quality inherent in our own natures. Possibly from his Manichean past, Augustine had a lifelong suspicion of matter and the flesh and saw human nature as essentially corrupt. He was suspicious of our ability to achieve deification from this corrupted flesh by our own means and so championed the power of God's grace over any 'Pelagian' notions of what we would nowadays refer to as 'original blessing'. In this respect the body of Christ on earth, the Church, remained the *sine qua non* for reaching the state of bliss denied us by our nature. Although glimpses of this could be afforded in this life, the true union would not be possible for Augustine in this world. As he states at the outset of the *Confessions*: 'the house of my soul is too small for you to enter, make it more spacious by your coming. It lies in ruins: rebuild it.'[63]

Thus confession, as a means to a purification of the memory (as one of the key constituent parts of the soul), becomes for Augustine from here on key to his insight into our ultimate connection with the divine, especially as located within the Church on earth.

SUMMARY: MIND, MEMORY AND TRUTH

By concentrating on the work of Augustine and the desert elders it is possible to draw a picture of the early Christian community beginning to appreciate the importance of confession as a means of expression of their essential Christian identity. On the one hand, the desert elders concentrated on what we would today call the psychological aspects of the practice as a means of developing a deeper understanding of our motivations and attitudes to the divine and our fellow humanity. Augustine, on the other hand, while not eschewing the psychological value of the practice, places it within his wider theological anthropology of what humanity is and whither are directed its deepest longings. For him confession thus becomes one of the means whereby the transcendent dimension is restored to our human personhood.

At the heart of these early Christian practices of confession is to be found Christ's statements in John 8.31 and 3.21 that 'you shall know the truth, and the truth shall make you free' and that 'those who do what is true come to the light'. Yet Augustine subtly redacts the latter phrase when he writes in Book Ten of the *Confessions*: 'For behold You love the truth: "He who makes the truth comes to the light" (*ecce enim veritatem dilexisti, quoniam qui facit eam venit ad lucem*). I wish to do it in confession, in my heart before You, in my writing before many witnesses.'[64] As O'Donnell points out, for Augustine, the 'making of truth' by the speech act of confession is as important as the 'facts' of the confession itself. The act of confession, as we shall see later in figures such as Wittgenstein and Kierkegaard, is not just about expressing certain 'hidden' facts – making them public – but rather it is about 'the making of truth' by a performative speech act: 'Augustine is urgently concerned with the right use of language, longing to say the right thing in the right way.'[65]

As we move, in the next chapter, from this late classical period to the medieval age we will see how these various confessional strands developed by the desert elders and Augustine between them will be consolidated and deepened before separating again at the birth of the modern Western soul.

CHAPTER TWO

THE BIRTH OF CONFESSION AND THE TRISTAN WOUND

'At last Lord Tristan had himself carried into a boat apart on the shore; and lying facing the sea he awaited death, for he thought: "I must die, but it is good to see the sun and my heart is still high. I would like to try the sea that brings all chances ... I would have the sea bear me far off alone, to what land no matter, so that it heal me of my wound ..."'[1]

PENANCE IN THE EARLY CHURCH

We saw in the previous chapter how confession emerged in early Christianity as a melding of two practices. On the one hand there was the desert tradition of spiritual direction with its family resemblance to our contemporary twenty-first-century psychological schools – especially with its 'hermeneutic of suspicion' with regard to individual motivation and the stress placed on the need for all those who seek God to undertake the search in the company of another seeker. On the other hand, we saw in Augustine an acknowledgement of the unique locus of confession as the place where we can establish a relationship to the transcendent in our lives. From these two sources confession will thus slowly become the sacramental act that we recognize today in the Catholic Church where the transcendent encounters the immanent. Accordingly, in this chapter we shall take up the story of how this occurred and the events surrounding the thirteenth century, when the sacrament was codified within the canons of the Catholic Church.

In the Catholic context, the power of the Church to exercise the forgiveness of sin in response to the penitential act of the believer is traced back to Christ's exhortation to Peter and the apostles 'to bind or loose' what is on earth as in heaven,[2] reiterated in numerous sayings, such as the exhortation not to forgive seven times but 'seventy times seven times'.[3] As Karl Rahner points out,[4] the pre-existing Jewish communities whence early Christianity arose would have been familiar with the practice of excommunication or expulsion from the synagogue for grave sins. The Rules of the Qumran Community, for example, stipulate such penances for acts such as lying, obstinacy, impatience, blasphemy, anger and, even, 'guffawing foolishly' (for which the punishment is 30 days' penance).[5] The early church took seriously this notion of the communal nature of guilt and sin and the power of the whole community to witness to the transgressions of the individual. Just as Christ displays 'the authority on earth to forgive sins',[6] so the Church he founded took this authority on to itself, especially as manifest in its communal and ecclesial aspect as the 'Body of Christ'. The passage in John 20.22–23 where the risen Christ breathes the Holy Spirit on the assembled disciples and instructs them that 'if you forgive the sins of any, they are forgiven them; if you retain the sins of any, they are retained' was interpreted as the moment this power was transferred to the early church. From these roots grew the practice that confession, penance and absolution would continue and vouchsafe the gift of the Holy Spirit to the believer as they entered the community of Christians at baptism.

Early church writers such as the author of the *Shepherd of Hermas* (second century), Tertullian (*On Penitence*), Clement of Alexandria (*The Stromata*) and Origen (*Homilies on Leviticus*) all stress that such a 'reconciliation' can only happen once in the Christian's life, suggesting that the usual early Christian practice was to see confession as a once-only opportunity for reconciliation with God and the Church on earth. As Tertullian puts it:

> (God) has permitted the door of forgiveness, although it is closed and locked by the bar of Baptism, still to stand somewhat open. He placed in the vestibule a second penitence so that it may open the door to those who knock; only once, however, because it is already a second time ... it should also be in public not private.[7]

However, this one-off reconciliation might apply to all sinners, even if their sins included heresy, schism or fornication. In this respect Tertullian's comparison of confession to a plank thrown to a drowning man has perhaps become the most quoted metaphor developed at this period, used by St Augustine and the Council of Trent alike:

> Do thou, a sinner like myself – yes and a lesser one than I, for I recognise my eminence in evil – lay hold of it and grip it fast, as one who is shipwrecked holds

on to a plank of salvation (*ut naufragus alicuius tabulae fidem*). It will buoy you up when you are plunged into a sea of sin and bear you safely to the harbour of divine mercy.[8]

The ceremony attached to such confession and reconciliation with the body of the Church was often elaborate and very public, frequently involving the penitent wearing a distinctive dress, fasting and taking a particular part in the liturgy to finally receive the reconciliation of the Church through the laying on of a bishop's hands and the anointing of oil – often not until the end of one's life. Confession in this early church sense is thus very public, very ceremonial and very final. In Rahner's words, 'there is no trace of a "private" sacramental penance'.[9] In the West these public shows of sacramental penance gradually become associated with the observances of Lent, which begins with the public observance of the penitential rites by those who have sinned.[10] This is still attested by church ceremonies to mark the beginning of Lent to this day (such as the public distribution of ashes). This early form of public, one-off penance and confession thus persisted well into the late classical/early medieval period. The Synod of Toledo in AD 589 (Canon 11) still defends it, but gradually it came to be seen as more necessary for those who had caused public shame and scandal to the Church. By the fifth/sixth centuries such public penances had largely become a one-off action in preparation for death. As Dallen puts it: 'since it could take place only once in a lifetime and since it often had consequences for the remainder of the penitents' lives, people's distaste was understandable'.[11]

From the sixth century onwards, for reasons which commentators find hard to explain, in the Celtic lands of Britain and Ireland a new form of penance and confession arose.[12] Various commentators have presented theories as to why from this period onwards individual personalized confession and absolution took hold among these peoples. As Dallen points out, however, there were significant differences between monastic confession as it arose in the British Isles during these early centuries and what would later be accepted by the Western church at the Fourth Lateran Council as the universal practice of personal confession. Both held in common that there was a 'tariff' by which the 'amount of sin' could be measured out and penance given. However, the Celts had no ritual in their system to mark the penitent's return to grace within the Church.[13] For Dallen, the Celts and Anglo-Saxons had 'a fear and anxiety regarding the supernatural' which 'expressed itself in a preoccupation with demons and fairies and the like'.[14] Which, to this (Celtic-origin) reader at least, seems a bit far-fetched. A little more convincing, as Dallen concurs, is the suggestion of the influence of the desert tradition of spiritual direction, which we examined in the previous chapter, on the practices and shape of the Celtic church.

Accepting that the Celtic church was focused largely upon monastic foundations and that the desert form of individual spiritual direction was prevalent there, it is accordingly not so difficult to explain the origins of this form of confession as an outgrowth of spiritual direction as practised among these monastic communities. The clear links between the Celtic and Eastern churches, not least geographical through shared sea routes, and the ongoing tradition of the East to allow Christian leaders other than bishops, in some cases lay-people and monks, to give forgiveness of sins,[15] suggests that something of this Eastern spirit was clearly abroad in the Celtic church. This new Celtic form of forgiveness of sins, or absolution, was not confined to one specific occasion, or indeed one specific season such as Lent, and could be uttered by a priest or monk using a simple verbal formula.[16] By the eighth century it is clear that this new form of 'private' confession with its accompanying tariff of penances had spread throughout the whole of Western Europe, slowly replacing the more public penances of the older tradition.

1215 – THE CELTS TRIUMPHANT

Thus Catholic confession as we know it today was invented 800 years ago, in the year 1215 to be precise. In that year the church fathers of the West met at the church of St John Lateran in Rome and decided that the practice of individual confession as had crept down to Southern Europe from the Celtic fringes of the North and West should be adopted by the Western church. In the centuries and decades preceding the Council this new form of confession had taken hold of the Latin West: individual auricular confession to a priest who would then absolve the sins committed. This practice, so familiar to us today, would have been unknown to, among others, Augustine, who would have been more acquainted with the notion of general absolution of sins in public ceremonies described previously.

From the Celts, then, who would spread their system throughout Europe as they practised their missionary zeal, the notion of individual spiritual direction allied to a tariff for individual sins committed began to emerge and take the place of the older Roman communal and liturgically based absolution. What cannot be found in the Celtic system, however, is a notion of a ritual of absolution allowing the penitent to be restored to the bosom of the flock of Christ. Thus, by the time the church fathers met in 1215 to codify various ecclesiastical practices, they were faced with a situation where the Celtic-monastic form of individual penance, confession and spiritual direction had become popular in most of the domains of the Western church while the old form of public liturgical penance and confession had become increasingly infrequent. Their work at the beginning of the century would be supplemented by that of the later scholastic theologians such as St Thomas Aquinas, Duns Scotus and the Victorines, who all discussed the nature and sacramentality of the forms of confession then in circulation within the Church, their arguments often focusing on the question of where the sacramentality of the process resided. Scotus had argued that the uttering of the words 'te absolvo' was essential for the sacramental validity of absolution, while Abelard suggested it lay in contrition. Thomas in the *Summa Theologiae* distinguishes between penance as a virtue and penance as a sacrament. For him, the parts of the sacrament were the penitent's acts (contrition, confession and satisfaction), thus creating for him a fusion in the sacrament between the personal and the public, taking his definition of 'sacrament' from St Gregory the Great: 'a sacrament consists in a certain ceremony in which the action is so performed that we take it to signify the sanctity it bestows'.[17] Therefore, in confession, 'the ceremony is so done that something holy is signified'. Two other aspects of Thomas' analysis of confession in the *Summa Theologiae* are also worth noting. First, reflecting the now widespread use of Celtic forms of penance, he argues that confession is not a one-off event but something that can be repeated throughout life.[18] Second, as he stresses the sacramentality of the act, he is at pains to distinguish 'two types of confession of sins': 'one is interior and is made to God. The other is outward confession of sins which is made to a priest.'[19] This split between sacramental and non-sacramental forms of confession will be one that will have long-reaching consequences for the Western notion of confession and the self in general, as we shall see shortly.

Thus, the culmination of all these medieval developments can be seen in Canon 21 of the Fourth Lateran Council, which stated:

All the faithful of both sexes shall after they have reached the age of discretion faithfully confess all their sins at least once a year to their own (parish) priest and perform to the best of their ability the penance imposed, receiving reverently at least at Easter the sacrament of the Eucharist, unless perchance at the advice of their own priest they may for a good reason abstain for a time from its reception; otherwise they shall be cut off from the Church (excommunicated) during life and deprived of Christian burial in death. Wherefore, let this salutary decree be published frequently in the churches, that no one may find in the plea of ignorance a shadow of excuse. But if anyone for a good reason should wish to confess his sins to another priest, let him first seek and obtain permission from his own (parish) priest, since otherwise he (the other priest) cannot loose or bind him.

The somewhat legalistic formula, stressing the need for annual confession for those who had 'reached the age of discretion', also paid homage to the older Celtic-monastic tradition of spiritual guidance by suggesting further that:

> The priest be discreet and cautious that he may pour wine and oil into the wounds of the one injured after the manner of a skilful physician, carefully inquiring into the circumstances of the sinner and the sin, from the nature of which he may understand what kind of advice to give and what remedy to apply, making use of different experiments to heal the sick one. But let him exercise the greatest precaution that he does not in any degree by word, sign, or any other manner make known the sinner, but should he need more prudent counsel, let him seek it cautiously without any mention of the person. He who dares to reveal a sin confided to him in the tribunal of penance, we decree that he be not only deposed from the sacerdotal office but also relegated to a monastery of strict observance to do penance for the remainder of his life.

The wound and physician metaphors are striking. The monastic tradition, as we have seen, had long emphasized this aspect of confession. The church fathers at the Lateran Council added to this the formulas of sacramentality, which will take confession into the next stage of its development. However, as this ecclesiastical form of confession developed, there was also a concomitant secular development, to which we turn next.

THE CONFESSIONAL SHIFT

The confessional shift of 1215 cannot be overstated, for at this point two rivers meet. In Dallen's words: 'the two ancient roles of spiritual counsellor and community official were thus combined in the person of the priest-confessor'.[20] As the role of the priest and authority figure increased, that of the lay-person and counsellor declined (although Aquinas still admits in the thirteenth century that sins can be confessed to a lay-person – even mortal sins – *in extremis*). Modern confession, as it emerged in the thirteenth century and focused on the priest-confessor, was one where both confession and absolution of sins were combined in the service of the sacrament. Although this simplified things from the canonical point of view, from a psychological perspective it had the effect of obscuring some key aspects of the confessional. In the previous chapter I suggested that confession contains two elements: an aspect that allows psychological healing, as described by Freud, Jung and their followers; and second, a 'window on to the transcendent', as described by Augustine. Once the psychological practice of confession became wedded to the Church's ability to bestow absolution of sins, from the thirteenth century onwards, these two elements merged together – which is to say that the element of confession that allows the healing of the soul became yoked to the canonical requirements of the sacrament.

Important though this is, this book seeks to explain the processes and purposes of confession from within and without the Church. What is striking from this point of view is that just as the Church codifies its reactions to a particular understanding of confession, penance and absolution in 1215, we can observe other movements growing in the Western *psyche* that seek to find this confessional aspect outside the Church. My argument here will be that this outgrowth will eventually find its way into what we may today call the 'psychological' dimension of confession. Before I explain what I understand by this, it may be worth recalling how such a psychological perspective may differ from the theological one we have explored so far.

WHAT DOES PSYCHOLOGY DO?

The words 'psychology', 'psychotherapy' and 'psychiatry' all have their roots in the Greek word *psychē / ψυχή*. As well as having attachments to the mysterious Greek goddess of that name, the original Greek word relates to a number of concepts that can be translated as *breath*, *bright*, *coloured*, *iridescent*, *moving*, *life*, *spirit* and even *butterfly*.[21] From this perspective, psychology can thus be defined as the *logos*, the conversation, about the *psyche*.

If the psyche is indeed 'iridescent and sparkling' like a butterfly, how then do we 'heal the butterfly' – be a *therapōs* of the *psychē*? If you have ever picked up a butterfly to release it from its prison in your house you will know the care required to transport it to freedom without damaging its gentle and fragile nature. This is the challenge that faces all who work with the *psyche*, whether they be confessors, counsellors, therapists, clergy, lay-healers, psychiatrists or spiritual directors. In seeking a mode of expression and analysis of this process, a helpful guide is the postmodern philosopher Ludwig Wittgenstein (1889–1951), to whom we shall turn in the next chapter. Commenting on the role of philosophy in the contemporary world, he stated:

> Philosophy may in no way interfere with the actual use of language; it can in the end only describe it. For it cannot give it any foundation either.
>   It leaves everything as it is.[22]

> Philosophy simply puts everything before us, and neither explains nor deduces anything. – Since everything lies open to view there is nothing to explain.[23]

Philosophy, like therapy or counselling, is for Wittgenstein a process of seeing correctly what lies before us.[24] So, in the case of our trapped butterfly, we don't have to prod and push it, but simply observe its movements, how it flutters, now this way, now that, until we can see at which point we can gently usher it towards its exit and freedom: 'What is your aim in philosophy? – To show the fly the way out of the fly-bottle.'[25]

When the American analyst Robert Johnson asked his mentor Fritz Kunkel how one went about learning psychology, Kunkel suggested three ways. First, to read all ancient mythology; second, to read the collected works of Carl Jung; and finally – and he felt this to be the best – to 'watch and wait'.[26] What does he mean by this? Again, Ludwig Wittgenstein throws some interesting light on this.

For him, the therapist and counsellor – like the philosopher – are not so interested in propounding theories and explanations as they are in observing the 'foundations of possible buildings', which will require a certain 'clarity of vision':

> Clarity, perspicuity (*Durchsichtigkeit*) are an end in themselves. I am not interested in constructing a building, so much as having a clear view (*durchsichtig*) before me of the foundations of possible buildings. My goal, then, is different from the scientist and so my think-way is to be distinguished.[27]

The observer and healer of the *psyche* – the psychologist – therefore sensitively observes the choreography of the *psyche* and spirit as they skate on the surface of the mysterious, the unknown (*unheimlich*), Freud's 'unconcious world'.[28]

Following this line of argument, the therapist, counsellor or spiritual director is therefore not a second-rate scientist or empiricist but is working from a different 'world view'. One, as Wittgenstein states, where 'all possible world views' are held in balance. The therapist is allowed an insight into all world views and then presents them to the listener. In this respect Wittgenstein saw the value of Freud's contribution to our understanding of the mind as being the observations not of a pseudo-scientist but of someone who 'changes the perspective' of their interlocutor. Following this thought-way, to which we shall return in the next chapter, a key point I would like to suggest is that we should view the practice of psychology as unlike other modes of healing, in particular, scientific-based modes.

There is a tendency today to relate counselling to scientific and observable, quantifiable and empirical 'outcomes'. As Robert Johnson says:

> When people enter therapy today with (a hunger for the divine) many healthcare professionals try to talk them out of their experiences; too many mainstream therapists pathologise the client's dreams and visions and make every attempt to get this neurotic individual back into the humdrum world of so-called 'normality'.[29]

Although no doubt of importance, such positions may obscure the fact that psychotherapy and counselling are themselves modes of operation other than and in many ways alien to the operations of the dividing and cutting cognitive mind. They are more at home in the *unheimlich*: that which is 'not at home' – that which is ushered in by the strange and inexplicable phenomena from the 'meadows of the underworld'. In this respect, I would argue, the successful therapist or counsellor is closer to the artist and poet than to the scientist or analytical investigator. Freud and Jung understood this despite Freud's attempts to put his nascent discipline on a more 'objective' and 'scientific' footing.[30] This seems to have wrong-footed later commentators. With the benefit of hindsight we could conclude by saying that counselling and psychotherapy owe more to the realm of myth-making than to scientific observation, and how we understand that will depend on our view of the value of *mythos* in a world increasingly obsessed by the emergent dominance of the *logos*. As the Western world seems to stumble from one existential, psychological and sociological crisis to another, I am reminded of the words of the Bengali Nobel Laureate Rabindranath Tagore, who wrote towards the end of his life: 'The spectre of a new barbarity strides over Europe, teeth bare and claws unconcealed in an orgy of terror … the spirit of violence dormant perhaps in the psychology of the West has roused itself and is ready to desecrate the spirit of Man.'[31]

Yet if in our conversation regarding the *psyche* we take the myths of culture seriously, as Kunkel and Johnson suggested we should, it will become instructive to relate the psychological changes of a culture to a shift in its mythology. Such a shift occurred in the West exactly as the Lateran Council was formulating its doctrine of confession in the first decade of the thirteenth century. This mythological world, known today through the 'Arthurian legends', received its first formal codification in the form by which we know it at this time. It is to this other innovation of the thirteenth century that we therefore turn next as we seek to understand the psychological role of confession in the modern soul.

THE SEA THAT BRINGS ALL CHANCES …

While the church fathers were at their deliberations in Rome a seemingly unconnected event was happening in Northern Europe: a German writer, Gottfried von Strassburg, was putting the finishing touches to his lengthy poem based on an old Celtic story – the legend of Tristan and Isolde.

One of my arguments in this book is that the two events are not so unconnected as may appear at first sight. If we view the events of the first decades of the thirteenth century through this filter we can begin to see that eight hundred years ago the Western *psyche* drank deeply of a love-philtre from which it has yet to recover. This love-philtre has continued to define the Western sense of wounding, guilt, sin and their mode of healing – confession. Yet, as with so much medieval symbology, we have lost the lodestone or key and fail to realize any longer that the answers to our desires lie in the sacrament which was established to restore a sense of peace lost by what I shall call here the 'Tristan wound'.

What, then, is this wound and how does it relate to confession?

I have argued so far in this book that confession contains two essential axes: a vertical moment whereby the act, as Augustine suggests, connects us with the divine and the transcendent; and a horizontal plane upon which, psychologically speaking, the act of telling others our secret fears and worries enables psychological release, as described by Freud and Jung in the previous chapter. In the early decades of the thirteenth century these two elements finally go their separate ways. The Church will take on to itself the sacramental and transcendent function of confession, codifying it in the canons of 1215, while the psychological verisimilitude of the act will be set adrift to float through the secular imagination. The havoc this will wreak is nicely told in the Tristan myth, where we see the first encounter of the psychological power of confession without its concomitant transcendent counterpart. This festering 'Tristan wound' remains as painfully unhealed today – daily to be re-encountered in every love affair, counselling room and secular occasion of confession as it was in 1215. Accordingly let us look at the Tristan myth, as told by Gottfried, and what it can tell us about the psychological nature of confession.

THE TRISTAN STORY

As I have argued so far, myth can be perceived as the doorway into the *psyche*, and as we listen to the ancient Tristan story it is possible to connect with those aspects of the modern *psyche* that remain unhealed today. The first thing to note is the name of the hero of our legend: 'Tristan', literally, 'the sad one'. Conceived from the sad union of Rivalin and Blanchefleur, the baby was born just as his mother died, his father having previously died in battle. He is thus the child of sorrow, an orphan. As the priest asks for the name of the child at his christening service, his guardian, the Marshal Rual li Foitenant, declares:

> 'In view of what I have heard from his father – his experience with his Blancheflor, the great sorrow in which her desire for him was assuaged, in what sorrow she conceived her child, and the sorrow with which she bore him – let us call him "Tristan".' Now Tristan means 'sorrow' and because of all these happenings the child was named 'Tristan' and christened 'Tristan' at once. His name came from 'triste'.[32]

Thus the first thing to note from the myth is that we modern souls are orphans. Our good Christian parents have died and we are born alone in the world. As Robert Johnson writes:

Tristan is the new child, born in the Middle Ages, who grew up over a millennium to be modern Western man. His mother and father, Blanchefleur and King Rivalin, symbolise the old order, the ancient mind of Europe. They die, but they give birth to a child and that child is the modern mind of the West. He is Tristan, the New Man.[33]

For Johnson, from his Jungian perspective, the death of the old order is the death of the feminine: 'she (Blanchefleur) personifies the inner feminine soul of Western man, the feminine values that once lived in our culture. Her death records that sad day in our history when our patriarchal mentality finally drove the feminine completely out of our culture and out of our individual lives.'[34] Although I admire much in Johnson's analysis, I am not so drawn to his perspective on the birth of Tristan as the death of the feminine. Rather, from the perspective of this book, I see the birth of Tristan as the death of the transcendent perspective at the birth of secular culture. In this respect I agree with Johnson when he characterizes us moderns as 'the children of sadness'; we are, he says:

children of inner poverty, though outwardly we have everything. Probably no other people in history have been so lonely, so alienated, so confused over values, so neurotic. We have dominated our environment with sledgehammer force and electronic precision. We amass riches on an unprecedented scale. But few of us, very few indeed, are at peace with ourselves ... Most of us cry out for meaning in life, for values we can live by, for love and relationship.[35]

As I stated at the beginning of this book, week after week I see the children of sadness who live in the West. Shorn of meaning, we live the life of 'triste'. And as Johnson points out, this alienation, this 'cut-off-ness', extends to all elements of our dealing with reality, especially the environment. In his ground-breaking encyclical, *Laudato Si'*, Pope Francis characterized this tendency as our present 'throwaway culture' and our worship of 'rapidification'.[36] Like Saint John Paul II, he critically analyses 'progress and our human abilities'[37] and the unholy 'alliance between the economy and technology' which 'ends up sidelining anything unrelated to its immediate interests'.[38] Within this critique (always of course within the spirit of dialogue and respect) there is even a critique of the scientific method itself ('a method of control'), which should not be allowed to assume the divine right to have the last word on every matter. For, in contrast to the mechanizing objectification of the scientific-economic gaze, the Pope advocates a vision of each creature that respects its creatureliness. 'Each creature', he states, 'has its own purpose', and in this he echoes the ancient church tradition which goes back to the desert elders of God being found in the 'book of creation' which we read by engaging in contemplation ('God has written a precious book').[39] This precious book of creation is therefore not just for aesthetic consideration but contains the full biodiversity of all creatures, the loss of which, as with all the other events cited, affects us all.[40]

Thus, the 'child of woe' is born into a world torn apart – alienated from itself and the sources of creation around it. The young Tristan must first engage in 'the study of books and language',[41] which is for him 'the beginning of cares', for:

> In the blossoming years, when the ecstasy of his spring-time was about to unfold and he was just entering with joy into his prime, his best life was over; just when he was beginning to burgeon with delight the frost of care (which ravages many young people) descended on him and withered the blossoms of his gladness.[42]

Where has childhood gone? In the frost of care our young ecstasy is quenched by the technocratic society within which we live, for 'he was learning the whole time, today one thing, tomorrow another, this year well, next year better'.[43] Our technocratic society demands this constant 24-hour learning made worse by the demands of the internet to which the young *psyche* is now glued.

Unfortunately, a *psyche* such as ours, unhinged from its transcendent moorings, is more susceptible to corruption, distraction and ruin, and in the next stage of the saga we hear that the young Tristan preoccupies himself with all the distractions available to the medieval lad: peregrines, games, fine silks and the hunt. Again our technologically obsessed age has brought all the distractions one could possibly imagine into the heart of our lives. Twitter, Facebook, social media and computer games could fill up our whole day should we allow them.

During this period of adolescent distraction (we are told he is 14 years old) the first of many strange incidents connected with the sea occurs to Tristan. At the mention of the sea a psychologist's ears prick up. 'The sea that brings all chances' is almost a character in itself during the Tristan saga. As the saga originates from the Atlantic isles surrounded by the constant ebb and flow of the sea and the flickering uncertain light of the coast, it would be strange if the sea itself did not play a significant role in the drama, yet the sea seems to fulfil a deeper function within the story. Johnson, following Jung, takes it as a symbol for the unconscious, 'our nostalgia for the mysterious, unexplored depths of our own psyches, for the hidden potentialities within our own souls: for what we have never known, never lived, never dared'.[44] Thus, as in the Parzifal legend,[45] we have in this story a record of our first adolescent encounter with the unconscious, at the age set by the Lateran Council 'as the beginning of discernment', normally understood as 14. As with Parzifal's encounter with the transcendent at that age, so Tristan must come to terms with the unconscious. Like his fellow seeker Parzifal, however, he also makes a mess of it.

What happens? One morning a bright merchant's ship arrives in Brittany from Norway. Tristan, his guardian Foitenant and his tutor, Curvenal, are invited on to the ship, where Tristan is distracted by a beautiful chessboard. Distracted as any youngster today would be by an Xbox or computer console, he challenges the Norwegians to a game and becomes completely absorbed by it. Like that other story, the *Sleeping Beauty*, where the adolescent cannot focus on the task before her but falls into a hundred-year sleep, so the boy Tristan denies what is happening and observes only the game before him. Two things now occur: his guardian, the Marshal, gets bored with the adolescent game and leaves the ship, while the Norwegians look on the boy and realize 'they have never set eyes on any young person with so many talents'.[46] Eyeing the boy for potential exploitation, they abduct him by letting slip the anchor so that the ship sails off with the boy and his tutor – both being so engaged in the game that they fail to notice what is happening until it is too late. So, Tristan's first encounter with the ocean/unconscious is a disaster – he is carried off into a very dangerous and hostile situation. With our present-day heightened awareness of child abuse, especially of teenagers, Tristan's fate seems eerily prescient. Fortunately for the boy, a storm is now raised in the ocean/unconscious. The deeper forces of the unconscious have been roused and for eight days they roll the ship, so much so that the Norwegians, terrified, agree to land the boy on the nearest shore that beckons: Cornwall.

The topography of the story of Tristan is worth noting. There are essentially three loci for the action. Brittany, the land of Tristan's birth, and Cornwall, the land of his young manhood, are the places of masculine power and patriarchy. This is the wounded martial land of the modern world, dominated by warfare, patriarchal codes and distance from the intuitive and creation. On the other side of the ocean, to which Tristan will eventually have to go, lies Ireland, ruled by the sorceress Queen Iseult. For the purposes of the myth, Ireland is the place of the unknown, the irrational, the uncontrollable. It is the place that Sigmund Freud will set out to explore in the late nineteenth century from his small flat on the Berggasse in Vienna and to which we shall return later. For once Tristan lands at Cornwall he finds that he is in the realm of his uncle, King Marke. Here his patriarchal and intellectual side can develop to the full and he takes to the court with gusto, as any young lad would. However, Cornwall is a land that lies in unease, as does our modern world. For every four years it must send a tribute of young boys and girls to be deflowered in Ireland (again, we have shadows of the layers of dark sexual abuse that lie hidden in our contemporary world). To gain this tribute Morold, the brother of the Queen of Ireland, arrives in Cornwall. The folk of Cornwall are too frightened to challenge him, but Tristan alone stands out and offers to challenge Morold to hand-to-hand combat. They fight on a small islet off Tintagel in full view of the crowd. The struggle is mortal and Tristan triumphs; however, he receives a wound, 'an ugly blow through the thigh, plunging almost to the very life of him, that his flesh and bone were laid bare'.[47] This wound is not just a mortal wound, it is a poisoned wound, as Morold had his sword tempered by the secret poisons of his sister.

Tristan is wounded, the wound with which we began this chapter, yet he is victorious. Morold is killed and the people of Cornwall rejoice. The great masculine hero has triumphed – but at what cost? As the rejoicing continues Tristan starts to ail:

> What then? The doctors were summoned, they applied their whole command of the art of medicine to him. Where did it get them and what was the use of it? He was not a whit better for it. Their whole assembled knowledge of medicine was of no advantage to him. The poison was such that they quite failed to draw it from the wound, till it suffused his whole body, which then assumed a hue so wretched that one scarcely

recognised him. Moreover, the place where the blow had fallen took on a stench so fearsome that life became a burden to him and his body was an offence. Further his greatest grief the whole time was the realisation that he was beginning to weigh upon those who, till now, had been his friends.[48]

This then is the Tristan wound, the wound I have argued in this book that we all possess. It is the wound that can only be healed by the transcendent, and if it is not, then it just festers and stinks. It lies close also to the sources of sexuality and *eros* as Tristan, like his Jewish forebear Jacob, is wounded in the thigh near to the sexual centres of the body. The patriarchal has triumphed, but at what cost? By its alienation from the transcendent it must now suffer in poisonous woe. Yet, the legend tells us, there is a solution – there is an antidote for the poison. This lies in a return to the ocean – the unconscious: 'I would like to try the sea that brings all chances … I would have the sea bear me far off alone, to what land no matter, so that it heal me of my wound'.[49] 'He accordingly', we are told, 'fixed his resolve on going to Ireland of all places … whatever fate God might hold in store for him in order to be cured.' Under cover of darkness, he is taken down to the shoreline and cast off on to the sea alone, with only his harp for company, but with no sword. To come to the place of healing he must cast off all the accoutrements of patriarchy and rely solely upon the instruments of unconscious intuition – the harp. For if we all possess the Tristan wound, we all deep down know where the answer lies – in the unconscious, the unknown, the letting go of the rational. Yet the tragedy of

Tristan is that he has lost the way back to the transcendent. The transcendent wound that he possesses can only be healed by the encounter with the transcendent. Instead, he finds his (temporary) healing comes from the Queen's daughter – Isolde – who, while healing Tristan's wound, falls in love with him. We all know what happens next (not least thanks to Richard Wagner). Tristan is healed by Isolde, she discovers he is the murderer of her uncle and wants nothing more to do with him, yet she too is caught up in the love spell that catches Tristan. Isolde seeks to poison Tristan, but her faithful maid, Brangwyn, substitutes a love-philtre for the poison so that both Tristan and Isolde will find their way not back to their transcendent homes, but rather only into the seething, unending passion of romantic love. Likewise, I suggest, the modern *psyche* too easily substitutes romantic or sexual attachment for its true transcendent home. All the projections, torments, transferences and counter-transferences of romantic love will blind us to the transcendent home that we sought all along – often masked in the ocean of the unconscious.

THE TRISTAN LEGEND AND THE FATHER WOUND

At this point you may be asking, 'But why the Tristan legend?' To answer this I quote a story told by the American Franciscan, Fr Richard Rohr, about an incident that happened to him when he was giving a retreat in Peru. Here he encountered a sister who worked in Lima's central prison:

She described how, as Mother's Day was approaching during her first year there, the men in the prison kept asking her for Mother's Day cards. She kept bringing boxes and boxes of cards for the prisoners to send to mama, but she never seemed to have enough. So as Father's Day approached, she decided to prepare for the onslaught of requests by buying an entire case of Father's Day cards. But that case, she told me, is still sitting in her office. Not one man asked her for a Father's Day card. She couldn't even give them away.[50]

Rohr puts this distinctive behaviour (first noticed by the English psychologist Donald Winnicott in *Deprivation and Delinquency*) down to what he terms 'the Father Wound':

She realized then – and as she told me this story with tears in her eyes I realized it too – that most of the men were in jail because they had no fathers ... They had never seen themselves as sons of men who admired them, they had never felt a deep secure identity, they had never received that primal enthusiasm that comes from growing up in the company of a father.[51]

The Father Wound, he suggests, lies behind their disturbed and disturbing behaviour:

Whether they engage in macho games of physical fitness, sexual prowess or business success, they are trying to show themselves and others they have made it, that they are really men. But their continuous running from one accomplishment to another only proves that they have not made it and subconsciously they feel their own incompleteness.[52]

Citing Jean Vanier, the founder of the worldwide L'Arche communities, he suggests that almost every man in Western society suffers not only from some form of Father Wound but also from an 'unhealed and unwhole sexuality'[53] which bleeds in 'sexual violence towards women and homophobia toward other men'.

One of my contentions here (following authors such as Jung, de Rougemont and Johnson) is that the Celtic-Christian myths of the twelfth/thirteenth centuries spontaneously arise at the defining moment of the creation of a whole culture, in this case our culture – that of the West. And by the strange way that myths work ('An entire mythology is laid down within our language', according to Wittgenstein)[54] – as dreams work – they lay down the neuroses and obsessions that will haunt the resulting cultural matrix. Thus, the two strongest dramas – Parzifal and Tristan – concern a wound, a male wound, and the quest for its healing. We began the chapter with Tristan lying wounded in Cornwall, the stench filling the room such that people retched if they came near it. As Vanier, Rohr, Johnston and others contend, we are living today with the wounded Tristan – the boy born fatherless who seeks the healing of his father wound.

'The father wound', writes Rohr, 'is so deep and so all-pervasive in so many parts of the world that its healing could well be the most radical social reform conceivable.'[55] In response, Rohr suggests that we 'should dedicate some of our own father energies to reforming destructive patriarchal structures and to nurturing and healing the next generation of men'.

Tristan, the child born in woe, is therefore the representative, the symbol, of the lost modern soul. Born without a father and mother, he seeks affection and approval from his adopted father, King Marke of Cornwall. This leads to his duel with the Irish giant, Morold. Interestingly, the message of the myth resonates with the prescription presented by Rohr. The wounded Tristan must disembark by night to take 'the sea that brings all chances'. He must float wounded and without his sword, the source of phallic power, as he returns to the wounded feminine. If we listen to the voice of the Tristan legend again we hear we are being called to abandon our position of male discriminating power and to allow the unconscious to flow once again. The Tristan legend invites us to a Wittgensteinian 'change of aspect'.

Writers as diverse as de Rougemont and Johnson have noticed that the Tristan myth also arises at the birth of another key trope of the modern Western *psyche* – romantic love – the love of the troubadour and the court minstrel.[56] This poison of romantic love, says Johnson, courses through the later bloodstream of the Western *psyche* as strongly as the love-philtre that Tristan and Isolde blindly drink together. In our search for the transcendent we resort to the next best thing – erotic love and romance. Though a seductive drug, this will not, however, assuage the longing for the transcendent within us.

As stated, beginning with Carl Jung and then following on through his students such as Marie-Louise von Franz, James Hillman and Robert Johnson, many twentieth-century psychologists saw the 'mythic' texts of medieval Europe as offering a pre-modern insight into the Western *psyche* that underlies so many of our contemporary concerns. In this respect, I would see the contemporary 'search for the sacred' as a wider 'search for the Spirit' that haunts the Western mind from its inception in the High Middle Ages. If we study the texts of the Celtic legends carefully we have in microcosm a view of how the Western mind views the transcendent and clues as to how we can deal with the present 'psycho-spiritual crisis' within which we find ourselves. In this way we can develop another key theme of the present book: the use of the imagination and its role in the healing art of the therapist, counsellor and spiritual director.

In this respect the Tristan legend is instructive as it is directly concerned with wounding and healing – in particular, with the transcendental wounding of the Western *psyche* at the beginning of the modern age. Sadly, for the healing of that wound, the confessional as the door back to the transcendent has been cordoned off by ecclesiastical curtains. Its secular substitute – the counselling room – allows the process of confession to happen but in many cases keeps the possible door to the transcendent firmly closed. Like Tristan, the modern person must therefore languish on a sickbed, unable to find healing and unable to die. This is the unbearable state of the postmodern soul as described by Foucault in the previous chapter.

A WAY FORWARD?

This chapter has, perhaps, made depressing reading. I have suggested that the fork in the path of Western culture that occurs in the medieval period has created an unbridgeable sacred/secular divide in the Western imagination. On the one hand I have described the sacramental confession of the Western church which adopts the psychological practices of the early church to its transcendent end. On the other, I have painted the picture of the wounded secular soul, lying prone on its psychological couch sickening for the transcendent. Although it would clearly be foolish to ascribe all the ills of the present-day world to this split, there is no doubt that it contributes to some of the distorted, and frankly pathological, attitudes we observe in our present culture – to ourselves, to each other and to creation around us. What is clearly required is a reconciliation, especially a reconciliation with the transcendent.

I did not set out to write a book that simply pointed to the pathology of the contemporary person without suggesting a way forward or a solution to the problem – a means to achieve that reconciliation with the transcendent. Accordingly, for the rest of this book I will chart a way forward using the examples of three late Western figures who can show us a way towards the healing of this transcendent wound. In taking these three – Ludwig Wittgenstein, Henri Le Saux and John of the Cross – I wish to suggest a way in which the transcendent and psychological horizons of the confessional can reconnect. In reviewing the work of all three, I will concentrate on their own confessional practices and how they present a healing path for the wounded modern soul. Although all suffer from the 'Tristan wound' by three different, yet connected, means, they find the way back to the source of healing denied the ailing Tristan. It is to their stories we turn next.

CHAPTER THREE

WITTGENSTEIN'S
PHILOSOPHICAL CONFESSIONS

'Work on philosophy is — as frequently work in architecture is — actually more a work on oneself. On one's
own conception. On the way one sees things (and what
one demands of them).'

Ludwig Wittgenstein[1]

ESCAPE TO NORWAY

In 1936 the 47-year-old Ludwig Wittgenstein decided he
had to leave his life and loves in Cambridge and set off
alone to the Norwegian fjords. This was nothing new. In
1913, faced with the need to put his thoughts and life in
order and complete the manuscript he had been puzzling
over for years — that would later become the only book
published in his lifetime, the *Tractatus Logico-Philosophicus* —
he had again turned his back on Cambridge and made his
way to the remote villages of Norway. Here, just before
the great civilizations of early-twentieth-century Europe
were about to be torn apart by the First World War, he
found what he wanted: silence, solitude and the spar-
tan regime that would allow him to complete his first,

some would say greatest, work. Ray Monk in his biog-raphy[2] comments that this year in Skjolden, the village he eventually chose to settle in, was 'possibly the most productive of his life'. '*Then*', Wittgenstein commented later to his friend Basil Reeve, 'my mind was on fire!'[3] But, as always with Wittgenstein, the logical exercises that he pursued with the aim of completing his book were not to be distinguished from the 'work upon himself' that he felt was paramount, for, as he wrote to Bertrand Russell back in Cambridge: 'how can I be a logician before I'm a human being! *Far* the most important thing is to put my own house in order!'[4] Which was easier said than done. The young philosopher (he was 24 at the time) might well have been pushing forward what Russell called 'the next big step in philosophy',[5] but he clearly lacked the personal qualities, or indeed character traits, to 'put his house in order'. He wrote to Russell of dividing his time in Norway between 'logic, whistling, going for walks and being depressed',[6] and his letters to Russell reveal the depth of psychological disturbance to which he was prey:

> Every day I was tormented by a frightful *angst* and by depression in turns and even in the intervals I was so exhausted that I wasn't able to think of doing a bit of work. It's terrifying beyond all description the kinds of mental torment that there can be! It wasn't until two days ago that I could hear the voice of reason over the howls of the damned and I began to work again.[7]

All this psychological disturbance was to boil over when he lashed out at Russell in his letters:

We haven't been able and we shan't *ever* be able to talk about anything involving our value-judgements without either becoming hypocritical or falling out. *I think this is incontestable*; I had noticed it a long time ago; and it was frightful for me, because it tainted our relations with one another: we seemed to be side by side in a marsh.[8]

Russell was able to brush aside Wittgenstein's personal criticisms, as he wrote to Lady Ottoline Morrell: 'I dare say his mood will change after a while.'[9] But the spat had revealed a fundamental difference between Russell's and Wittgenstein's approach to philosophy: Russell, the consummate professional, was able, in Wittgenstein's view, to produce for his audiences 'cut and dried results' rather than (which was infinitely preferable for the Austrian) the account of his thought processes as they were occurring. For Wittgenstein there was 'a perpetual seething, like the bottom of a geyser' that lay at the bottom of his thought processes and which he hoped would erupt at some point and turn him 'into a different person'.[10] This would take more than a short stay in Norway to achieve.

Between that first visit to Norway in 1913 and his later one in 1936, Wittgenstein's, and his native Austria's, world would change irrevocably. The assassination of the heir to the Austro-Hungarian throne, the Archduke Franz Ferdinand, on 28 June 1914 fired the starting gun that plunged Europe into the Great War later that year. In an attempt to find 'the nearness to death which will bring light into life',[11] Wittgenstein enlisted in the Imperial and Royal Austro-Hungarian army on 7 August 1914, shortly after Austria-Hungary declared war against Russia. The initial stages of the war were seemingly quiet and much of Ludwig's time was spent on the battleship *Goplana* on the Vistula River, captured from the Russians early on in the war, and working in military workshops around Krakow and Lemberg. On 21 April 1916, however, he found himself in battle for the first time and at this point he remained on solitary duty at the observation post. On 4 June the Austrian offensive was followed by an equally severe Russian offensive. Wittgenstein clearly acquitted himself well during this hellish time and was awarded a silver *Tapferkeitsmedaille* Second Class on 6 October. His decoration commendation stated:

> Ignoring the heavy artillery fire on the casement and the exploding mortar bombs he observed the discharge of the mortars and located them … On the Battery Observation Post, Hill 417, he observed without intermission in the drumfire, although I several times shouted to him to take cover. By this distinctive behaviour he exercised a very calming effect on his comrades.[12]

As equally distressing, for the sensitive son of a *hochbürgerlich* Austrian family, was the time he had to spend in close proximity to the 'great unwashed' of the Austro-Hungarian army. Ordinary folk, whom he had first met at the *Realgymnasium* at Linz (including, notoriously, Adolf Hitler), were as stressful to him as the Russian enemy. As he wrote in his diary:

> Now I am almost always with people who hate me. And this is the one thing that I have never been able to

come to terms with. The people here are wicked and heartless. It is virtually impossible to find even a trace of humanity in them. God help me to live ... God be with me! Amen.[13]

The people I am with are not so much nasty as *terribly* limited. This makes relations with them almost impossible as they almost always misunderstand me. They are not stupid, but limited. Within their circles they are clever enough. But they lack character and with that a breadth of understanding. 'The right-believing heart understands everything.'[14]

By the time Wittgenstein was withdrawn from the front line in August 1916 he had been continuously in the firing line for five months. Of the notes made at this time McGuinness comments: 'they testify to a change in his thinking as great as that which he himself saw in his countenance ... It was as if he had bridged – or was about to bridge – some gap between his philosophy and his inner life.'[15] From this point onwards there is no separation between the remarks on logical form and those on religion and ethics in his private diaries: 'yes my work has broadened out from the foundations of logic to the essence of the world'.[16]

Both of his biographers, Monk and McGuinness, suggest that at this point in his life, having pushed himself hard on the logical boundaries of language both in Cambridge with Russell and on his own in his retreat in Norway before the outbreak of the First World War, it was as though he 'sought embodiment' and needed the experiences of the trenches to bridge gaps between how he experienced his

thought and how he experienced his life. In this respect
his experiences on the Eastern Front in 1916 are central
for understanding the move in his philosophy from the
disembodied exploration of logical form to the embodied
researches of the later (or perhaps better 'post-1916')
Wittgenstein. This will bear fruit in the final published
version of the *Tractatus* – a logical tract ending, notoriously, with Wittgenstein's comments on aesthetics, the
mystical and ethics.[17] The evidence for this change can be
found in the confessional remarks that he began to make in
his personal diaries from this period.

In addition to the embodying experiences that befell
young Ludwig at this time, an equally important intellectual influence was to impinge itself upon him: that of
the great nineteenth-century man of letters, Count Lev
Tolstoy. Russell, in a letter to Lady Ottoline Morrell in
1919, tells the strange story of how, shortly after arriving in Galicia during his war service in 1914, he walked
into a bookshop which only contained one book – Tolstoy's
Gospel in Brief.[18] At this time he was feeling particularly low
and in Monk's words he was quite literally 'saved by the
word'.[19] He carried it with him wherever he went for the
rest of his service and became known to his fellow troops
as 'the man with the gospels'[20]: 'he read it and re-read it,
and thenceforth had it always with him, under fire and at
all times'.[21] As Wittgenstein later wrote to von Ficker: 'if
you are not acquainted with it, then you cannot imagine
what an effect it can have upon a person'.[22]

On 5 September 1914, shortly after reading *The Gospel
in Brief*, he wrote that 'I am on the path to a great discovery,
But will I reach it?!'[23] Monk suggests that for Wittgenstein,

from this point onwards, 'sensuality and philosophical thought were inextricably linked – the physical and mental manifestations of passionate arousal'.[24] Whether it was from Tolstoy or his war experiences, something had clearly happened to influence the development of the young philosopher profoundly.

In his exposition of Tolstoy, Sontag[25] notices the similarities between Tolstoy's relation to Christianity and the position Wittgenstein will ultimately adopt to philosophy. Both want to 'leave everything as it is' and allow the Scriptures/ordinary language to speak for themselves. Tolstoy, like Søren Kierkegaard, argues that Christianity must be stripped down to its essentials, leaving each person to make their own decision on its truth uninfluenced by the rhetoric and opinions of the churches.

As Wittgenstein was making his acquaintance with Tolstoy's writings, he also met a friend whose reminiscences have given us valuable insights into the state of Wittgenstein's soul at this traumatic time. Paul Engelmann (1891–1965), born in Olmütz, where Wittgenstein met him while stationed there in 1916, had been a student of Adolf Loos in Vienna (as well as secretary to Karl Kraus) and was to become a lifelong friend and confidant of Wittgenstein. Reflecting later on the relationship between Wittgenstein and Tolstoy, he commented that Wittgenstein's religious views 'led to an attitude to life that comes nearest perhaps to that sought by Tolstoy: an ethical totalitarianism in all questions, a single-minded and painful preservation of the purity of the uncompromising demands of ethics, in agonising awareness of one's own permanent failure to measure up to them'.[26]

Reading the first lines of Tolstoy's *Gospel* again, it is not surprising that it had such an explosive impact on Wittgenstein after his logical odyssey in Cambridge and Norway during the pre-war years. The words could have been Wittgenstein's own:

> Reason without faith had already brought me to despair and to a denial of life, but when I once really examined into the life of humanity, I became convinced that despair cannot be the destiny of man, and that people have lived, and are now living by faith …
>
> I tried to arrange my life after the lives of those who believe, tried to become one with them, to fulfill the same rules of life and laws of conduct, imagining that in this way the idea of life would be revealed to me also.[27]

Tolstoy continues: 'At first I sought counsel and a solution to my difficulties from priests, monks, bishops and learned theologians. But I often noticed in them a want of frankness, and still more frequently flagrant self-contradictions in their explanations and interpretations.'[28]

Tolstoy, like Wittgenstein, describes in his writings a movement from intellectual abstraction to pragmatic engagement in the world around him and, as it would later be for Wittgenstein, the act of confession would be a key catalyst for that transition. Tolstoy would describe this transformation in his 1879 essay *My Confession*, which it is hard to imagine Wittgenstein did not become acquainted with after his return from the Eastern Front.[29]

Like Augustine, and so many of our confessors, Tolstoy begins his confession by describing the dissolution of his youth and his turn away from God and religion, prompted in his case by his sceptical contemporaries. His 'abominable passions', he tells us, were praised and encouraged: 'ambition, lust for power, selfishness, voluptuousness, pride, anger, revenge'[30] led to 'lying, stealing, acts of lust of every description, drunkenness, violence, murder – there was not a crime which I did not commit'.[31] This mayhem continued, he tells us, for a decade as a young man before, in middle age, he began to mull over his indiscretions. For at this time, 'something strange began to happen to me: I was overcome by minutes at first of perplexity and then of an arrest of life, as though I did not know how to live or what to do, and I lost myself and was dejected'.[32] These 'minutes' grew longer and longer, prompting him continually to ask the questions 'Why? Well, and then?' By these means his 'life came to a standstill' for 'what happened to me was that I, a healthy, happy man, felt that I could not go on living … the thought of suicide came as naturally to me as had come before the ideas of improving life'.[33] At fifty years old he asked himself the questions: 'Why live, wish for anything, why do anything?' 'Is there in my life a meaning which would not be destroyed by my inevitable, imminent death.' In this state he records finding no help in science, philosophy or any of the great world faiths: Buddhism, Islam, Orthodox Christianity or Protestantism.[34]

At a logical dead-end, like Wittgenstein in 1914, Tolstoy tells us he ultimately found what his heart sought through 'the acquaintance of the believers from among the poor, the simple and unlettered folk, of pilgrims, monks, dissenters, peasants'.[35] These, he tells us, helped to relieve him from 'the error of rational knowledge'.[36] By listening to 'the conversation of an illiterate peasant, of a pilgrim, about God, about faith, about life, about salvation'[37] he experienced a return from the brink of suicide and a restoration in his faith in a God. Yet, unlike his childhood view of religion, this was a God beyond 'the concept of God', for 'the concept of God is not God'.[38]

THE RETURN TO EXPERIENCE

Tolstoy's return to experience, and ultimately the confessional, was what would also mark the second phase of Wittgenstein's philosophical career – what has become known as the 'later Wittgenstein' – and much in Tolstoy's confession quoted above would find a home in Ludwig's heart during the rest of his life.

Thus the Wittgenstein who was demobbed in 1918 was a changed man – having undergone these life-changing experiences, he was no longer the young logician who had left Cambridge and fled to Norway some four years earlier. His questing spirit, the circumstances of the war and the encounter with Tolstoy had all led him to see the necessity for a form of knowledge that was not just 'head knowledge' but rather the embodied knowledge which Tolstoy describes, coalescing in Wittgenstein's case around the need for complete honesty in the approach to his own personal affairs with others. As Engelmann would later observe: 'what prompted him was an overpowering – and no doubt long-suppressed – urge to cast off all encumbrances that imposed an insupportable burden on his attitude to the outside world: his fortune as well as his necktie'.[39]

It is not surprising, then, that after his war experiences the next decade of the philosopher's life would be spent in self-searching – largely avoiding the pursuit of logic and academic philosophy – and forming acquaintances with 'the poor, simple and unlettered folk'. Having renounced his not inconsiderable family fortune, during the next decade he worked as a monastery gardener, a school-teacher for infants in the Lower Austrian backwaters and an architect commissioned to build his sister's new house in Vienna (in collaboration with Paul Engelmann), even at one stage considering becoming a priest himself so that he could 'have read the Bible with the children'.[40] In Monk's words, 'he was faced with the task of re-creating himself – of finding a new role for the person that had been forged by the experiences of the last five years'.[41]

During this post-war period, as he battled depression and suicidal thoughts, he received an interesting letter from Engelmann, who was likewise suffering from the strains of what we would now call Post-Traumatic Stress Disorder. After a period (like Wittgenstein's) away from his family on retreat in the countryside, Engelmann wrote:

I did something about which I can tell *you*, because you know me well enough not to regard it as a piece of stupidity. That is, I took down a kind of 'confession,' in which I tried to recall the series of events in my life, in as much detail as possible in the space of an hour. With each event I tried to make clear to myself how I should have behaved. By means of such a general over-see (*übersicht*) the confused picture was much simplified. The next day, on the basis of this newly-gained insight, I revised my plans and intentions for the future.[42]

Perhaps Engelmann's example (no doubt supported by subsequent conversations) lodged itself in Wittgenstein's mind, and as he sought to drag himself through these difficult post-war years, in particular struggling with 'not being able to get over a particular fact',[43] Engelmann's wise support became essential.

In 1929 he finally returned to academic philosophy as a lecturer at Cambridge. (As John Maynard Keynes acerbically reported it to Lydia Lopokova in a letter: 'Well, God has arrived, I met him on the 5.15 train.')[44] He was, however, a changed man. Gone was the young Wittgenstein who had regularly jousted with Russell and been courted by the Bloomsbury group; instead Cambridge was faced with the middle-aged traumatized ex-soldier fired by Tolstovian zeal to 'work upon himself'. As he attempted to do this in the bourgeois setting of inter-war Cambridge (with many famous and amusing anecdotes), he was led once again to his beloved Norway to seek the solitude and silence that had worked its magic two decades previously. But Ludwig at 47 was not Ludwig at 24 and the effect, as well as the consequences, of this last stay in Norway was very different from that of the earlier one. As a young man he had been inspired to new heights of logical expression that would form the basis of the epic *Tractatus*; a quarter of a century later, his musings were to take him in a different direction that lies at the heart of this present book – towards the confessional.

ALL PHILOSOPHY BEGINS WITH A CONFESSION

Before he set out for Norway in August 1936 Wittgenstein had already tried to formulate his latest thoughts in two sets of writing, one later published as the *Brown Book,* and a set of reflections published as *Remarks on Frazer's Golden Bough.*[45] The *Remarks*, in particular, reveal themes that will haunt Wittgenstein during his year in Norway. He begins them by stating:

> One must begin with error and lead it towards the truth.
>
> That is, one must reveal the source of error other-wise hearing the truth will do us no good. The truth cannot break in when something else is taking its place.
>
> To convince someone of the truth it is not sufficient just to state the truth but one must find the *way* from error to truth.
>
> I must continually plunge myself into the water of doubt.[46]

Once again we are at the place where we began this book – the place of unknowing at the centre of the self where, like Wittgenstein in Norway, we have to plunge 'into the water of doubt' as we 'work on ourselves'. In the early pre-war notebooks he had kept in Norway the notes on the two processes of logical speculation and personal growth had occurred side by side. Now, returning as an older man, he was finally able to forge the two together, and the outcome of his stay would subsequently form the first 188 paragraphs of his last great posthumously printed work, the *Philosophical Investigations* (about a quarter of the book). As Monk writes of this period, it was a time 'when he was most ruthlessly honest about himself – when he made the most intense efforts to "descend into himself" and admit to those occasions on which his pride had forced him to be deceitful'.[47] It is perhaps no coincidence, then, that both the *Remarks on Frazer's Golden Bough* and the *Philosophical Investigations* begin with reflections on the *Ur*-text of Western confession: St Augustine's *Confessions*. 'Was Augustine then in error', he wrote at the beginning of the *Remarks*, 'when he called on God on every page of the *Confessions?*',[48] while the *Investigations* famously begins with an extended quote from the *Confessions*:

> When they (my elders) named some object, and accordingly moved towards something, I saw this and I grasped that the thing was called by the sound they uttered when they meant to point it out. Their intention was shewn by their bodily movements, as it were the natural language of all peoples: the expression of the face, the play of the eyes, the movement of other parts of the body, and the tone of voice which expresses our state of mind in seeking, having, rejecting, or avoiding something. Thus, as I heard words repeatedly used in their proper places in various sentences, I gradually learnt to understand what objects they signified; and after I had trained my mouth to form these signs, I used them to express my own desires.[49]

As Monk comments, 'for Wittgenstein *all* philosophy, in so far as it is pursued honestly and decently, begins with a confession'.[50] For Wittgenstein, this confession would

begin with his own notebook – the private diary that he
had kept from his days in the trenches and which traced,
as we have seen, all the moods and seasons of his emotions
and thoughts as they grew.

The publication and availability of these confessional
notebooks has been patchy since his death in 1951. His
literary executors saw their priority as getting as much of
his 'purely philosophical' work published and in the public
domain as quickly as possible. One of the unintended
consequences of these early publications was that the
general reading public got the overall impression that this
passionate, tormented man was a somewhat cold, detached
logician. Elizabeth Anscombe, one of his literary executors,
remarked that, 'if by pressing a button it could have been
secured that people would not concern themselves with his
personal life, I should have pressed that button'.[51] Another
of his executors, Georg Henrik von Wright, states in the
preface to the 1977 edition of the *Vermischte Bemerkungen*
(published in English in 1980 with the title *Culture and
Value*), extracted from Wittgenstein's private diary, that the
criteria for publishing his collection were as follows:

> In the end I decided on the only principle of selection
> that seemed to me unconditionally right. I excluded
> from the collection notes of a purely 'personal' sort –
> i.e. notes in which Wittgenstein is commenting on the
> external circumstances of his life, his state of mind
> and relations with other people – some of whom are
> still living. Generally speaking these notes were *easy* to
> separate from the rest and they are on a *different* level of
> interest from those which are printed here.[52]

The result of these early editorial decisions has been to reinforce the notion that his 'philosophy' could be extracted from his 'life'. This began to change towards the end of the twentieth century after the groundbreaking biographies of Monk and McGuinness shed new light on the interconnection between Wittgenstein's thought and life, augmented by the work of scholars such as Klagge[53] which has allowed much subsequent scholarship to reintegrate Wittgenstein's philosophical concerns with the context of his life. However, when scholars and executors began to pore over Wittgenstein's literary legacy, the *Nachlass*, they encountered a problem. Many of the entries were made in a secret code. These so-called secret diaries began during Wittgenstein's military service as a young man and continued throughout his life. They are interspersed among the 'open' entries and employ a simple code of replacing a with z, b with y, and so on. The first public edition of what became known as the 'Secret Notebook' was published in Spanish, Catalan and German in the Spanish journal *Saber* in 1985 edited by Baum and Pascual, and caused something of a stir. This text eventually appeared in a German-Spanish edition published by Alianza in Madrid in 1991.[54] Although no complete English translation of the 'Secret Notebook' has appeared to date, scholars such as Klagge have made extensive use of it in recent editions of, for example, the Norway diaries from the 1930s, and it is to this work, and the Bergen Electronic Edition of the complete *Nachlass*, that I will be making particular reference during this chapter as we explore the secret confessional of Wittgenstein's private journals and the impact this has on an understanding of not just the man but his philosophy.

A YEAR OF CONFESSIONS

Some of the first mentions of Wittgenstein's 'confessions' appear in his diary entries at Skjolden shortly after his arrival there in autumn 1936. Thus he comments on 19 November:

> About 12 days ago I wrote to Hänsel[55] a confession of my lie concerning my ancestry. Since that time I have been thinking again and again how I can and should make a full confession to everyone I know. I <u>hope</u> and <u>fear</u>! Today I feel a bit sick, frozen. I thought: 'Does God want to put an end to me before I could do the difficult thing?' May it turn out well![56]

The next day he continued:

> After having now made that <u>one</u> confession it is as if I couldn't support the whole edifice of lies anymore, as if it had to collapse entirely. If only it had entirely collapsed already! So that the sun could shine on the grass and the ruins.[57]

This reflects the entry later published in *Vermischte Bemerkungen*: 'the edifice of your pride is broken down. And that is terrible work.'[58] Thus from an initial confession about his supposed covert Jewishness, Wittgenstein felt the urge for a general confession, which duly appeared in the following days in a long letter addressed to his sister Hermine on 24 November[59] which contained instructions that the confession be shared among all the family. As he wrote to Hänsel: 'I lied to you and several others back then during the Italian internment when I said that I was descended one quarter from Jews and three quarters from Arians, even though it is just the other way round.'[60] Hänsel replied urging Wittgenstein to seek a Catholic priest for full Catholic confession (*Beichten*) and to try and find the Norwegian Catholic convert Sigrid Undset (1882–1949) to share this with.[61]

With respect to his own family and friends there is undoubtedly a tragicomic element in his attempts to make his general confession to them, well described by Monk in his biography.[62] What was conceived in the Nordic purity of his philosopher's hut did not necessarily play out in the way he had envisaged in the perfumed atmosphere of the Viennese salon. We hear that back in the Vienna home in Christmas 1936 Wittgenstein left the written confession on display for all to read in the reading room of the house; however, his sister Margarete thwarted his attempt for public disclosure by remarking that 'honorable people do not read another person's confession'.[63] Margarete herself wrote to Ludwig on 3 December 1936, just before he left Norway, that 'you surely know that to each of the sins you confessed I could juxtapose my own, or far worse ones of the same kind'.[64]

If the Viennese had problems with Ludwig's public penance then his English friends were even more uncomfortable with these unwished-for public displays, especially when, in the case of Rowland Hutt, they occurred in a corner of a Lyon's café delivered with Ludwig's crisp and clear tones for all and sundry to hear.[65] G. E. Moore and Maurice Drury heard the confession but never commented on its contents. Fania Pascal, on the other hand, found the whole episode slightly farcical and also found it difficult to react sympathetically. 'What is it? You want to be perfect?'

she challenged him, to which he replied, '*Of course* I want to be perfect.'[66] Commentators have often concentrated on the nature of the content of the confessions as delivered to these witnesses. Yet it is clear, reading back into Wittgenstein's Norwegian diaries when the confessional idea was conceived, that it was the *act* of the confession, as much as its *content*, that possessed him. Here we return to the thought-world of Augustine that we explored earlier. In common with many Christian saints, Wittgenstein seemed to suffer from scruples as he continually tried not to 'hoodwink' his listeners but to give them full exposure to all the flaws in his character, warts and all. Thus the debasing of himself, whether in the family reading room or in the Lyon's corner house, was an essential part of the confessional act for the philosopher. This, he felt, would counteract the perceived flaws in his character. Perhaps here we hear the echoes of those Benedictine monks with whom he had spent so much time over the past decade:

> My conscience presents me as a miserable human being to myself; weak, that is unwilling to suffer, <u>cowardly</u>: in fear of making an unfavourable impression on others, for example on the doorman at the hotel, the servant etc. Unchaste. Most heavily, though, I feel the charge of cowardice. But behind it stands indifference (and arrogance). But the <u>shame</u> I feel now is also no good insofar as I feel the outward defeat more strongly than the defeat of truth. My pride and my vanity are hurt.[67]

His catalogue of errors continued over many weeks and months, enumerating the many perceived instances of

arrogance, unchastity, cowardice, superiority and indiffer-
ence he felt himself guilty of over his lifespan. Worst of all
was the thought of describing all this to his lover and friend
Francis Skinner (1911–41) with whom he had been living
in Cambridge. Yet Francis wrote back on 6 December that
'whatever you say to me can't make any difference in my
love for you. I am terribly rotten in every way myself',[68]
and three days later he added: 'There won't be any question of my forgiving you as I am a much worse person than
you are. I think of you a lot and love you always.'[69]

That Wittgenstein had been miserable, both in 1913 and
now later in 1937, cannot be doubted. However, whereas
the young Ludwig had sought relief from his misery in
the coolly logical speculations of the *Tractatus*, the tactics
of the middle-aged man were slightly different. His war
experiences had swept away the pretence of compartmen-
talization that had haunted the young man. By contrast,
two decades later, all was to play for and 'nothing could
be hidden'. Rather than resolving the dilemmas of his
soul by acts of logic, the later Wittgenstein, a more embodied being than his former self, had to find his solution
through the performative act of confession with friends,
acquaintances and strangers alike – no matter how painful
or embarrassing (in a diary entry for 25 November 1936
he contemplates making his confession to the Norwegian
villagers around him, surely an echo of Tolstoy's path
described earlier).[70] 'I would like to be deep', he confides
to his diary on 16 February 1937, 'and yet I shy away from
the abyss in the human heart!!'[71] 'To know oneself is fearful
(*furchtbar*)', he writes on 15 March, as the long Norwegian
winter slowly comes to an end and the sun returns to his

log cabin, adding, 'for one knows the living demand and that one doesn't fulfil that demand.'

Yet out of these agonies, in contrast to the musings of his earlier self, glimmers of hope began to emerge, coinciding with the return of the watery northern sun. 'I am doing undeservedly well', he confesses to his 'secret' diary on 10 March,[72] as he seems to undergo a sea change in his agonizing speculations.

Almost a century later, poring over these diaries, secret and otherwise, and reading the words of his biographers and companions, it is of course futile to speculate as to what Wittgenstein had undergone during this crucial stage of his life, but that it would finally usher in his last great spell of philosophical creativity cannot be doubted. By May 1937 he had returned to Vienna and then Cambridge to meet with Francis and discuss the way forward in his life. This is the first record we have of the written typescript of the first 188 remarks of the *Philosophical Investigations*. Whatever else it had done, Wittgenstein's visit to the confessional seems to have unlocked the floodgates of his philosophical work. Considering the nature of the *Investigations*, and their stylistic difference from the *Tractatus*, this is perhaps unsurprising. More than most philosophers, for Wittgenstein the medium was often the message, and suddenly born, as if full grown, was the late style of Wittgenstein's writing that would intrigue, provoke and irritate readers thereafter. That teasing, self-questioning style doesn't just evoke the private confessional analysis that Wittgenstein had forced upon himself in the tormented days spent in his Norwegian log cabin in the 1930s, it also forces the reader to enact the confessional style upon themselves as they work through his puzzles, teases and jokes. Monk was right: not only did Wittgenstein's late philosophy begin with a confessional act but, I would argue here, if we engage deeply with his philosophy it will initiate the confessional act within us, his readers.

Therefore, one of the surprising consequences of Wittgenstein's confessions is that it forces us, his readers, to confessions of our own as we join him in our own examination of 'the abyss of the human heart'. As he makes clear in one of his later attempts to codify his philosophy – the so-called *Big Typescript* of 1932[73] – he sees the aim of philosophy as that which produces transformative change through working on *affect* as much as on *intellect*: 'a resignation, but one of feeling and not of intellect' that is required for 'work on philosophy is – as work in architecture frequently is – actually more of a kind of work on oneself. On one's own conception. On the way one sees things.'[74] As he states at the head of this manuscript, the 'difficulty of philosophy' is 'not the intellectual difficulty of the sciences but the difficulty of a conversion (*die Schwierigkeit einer Umstellung*). The resistances of the will must be overcome.'[75] Wittgenstein was to put this theory to the test in startling fashion during his 'year of confessions' in 1936/7. For as well as the private (and general) confessions he made to his family and friends concerning lies about his ancestry and his general character traits, he also confessed the specific instances of when he hit children whom he was meant to be teaching in Lower Austria a decade earlier. Fania Pascal remembers him saying:

During the short period when he was teaching at a village school in Austria, he hit a little girl in his class and hurt her (my memory is, without details, of a physically violent act). When she ran to the headmaster to complain, Wittgenstein denied that he had done it.[76]

During this year of conversion/confession he made the journey to Otterthal in Lower Austria specially to confess these sins to his erstwhile pupils.[77] One of them, Georg Stangel, later recalled in the 1970s:

> I myself was not a pupil of Wittgenstein's, but I was present when shortly before the war Wittgenstein visited my father's home to apologise to my brother and my father. Wittgenstein came at midday, at about one o'clock, into the kitchen and asked me where Ignaz is. I called my brother, my father was also present. Wittgenstein said that he wanted to apologise if he had done him an injustice. Ignaz said that he had no need to apologize, he had learnt well from Wittgenstein. Wittgenstein stayed for about half an hour and mentioned that he also wanted to go to Gansterer and Goldberg to beg their pardon in a similar way.[78]

Other villagers were less philosophical than little Ignaz and, according to interviews conducted among them by Adolf Hübner in the 1970s,[79] some were able to provide Wittgenstein with the necessary humiliation he clearly saw as part of the process of confession. Little Hermine Piribauer, the girl whose ears and hair he had pulled as a teacher, gave a curt 'Ja, Ja' response as he asked for forgiveness.

The 'year of confessions' – 1936/7 – was thus a key staging post in Wittgenstein's journey from 'error to truth' as he continually plunged himself 'into the water of doubt'.[80] Yet, and I think it is important to bear this in mind, this was not simply a personal journey of self-discovery for, as I have suggested here, for Wittgenstein the confessional act had a deeply philosophical hinterland, and the two acts – confession and philosophical speculation – were for him irrevocably intertwined. Consequently, in the remainder of this chapter I shall draw conclusions from Wittgenstein's confessional work not only for our understanding of the nature of confession but also for the impact this has on the act and work of 'doing philosophy', especially in the shadow of the Tristan wound we explored in the previous chapter.

WITTGENSTEIN AND PHILOSOPHICAL CONFESSION

In light of the above discussion I would like to conclude this chapter by suggesting three ways in which Wittgenstein's 'philosophical confessions' shed light on the nature and role of confession itself and its intimate bond to philosophical speculation.

1. Philosophy as therapy: 'work upon oneself'

After his 'year of confessions' Wittgenstein later recalled to his friend Rush Rhees:

Last year with God's help I pulled myself together and made a confession. This brought me into more settled waters, into a better relation with people, and to a greater seriousness. But now it is as though I had spent all that, and I am not far from where I was before. I am cowardly beyond measure. If I do not correct this, I shall again drift entirely into those waters through which I was moving then.[81]

For, as he had stated at the beginning of the *Big Typescript*, the heart of all philosophy lay in the 'conversion' that it produced. For him, the confessional held the key to the transformation of personality, the roots of which lay close to the sources of philosophy itself – 'the work upon oneself' that must be pursued to its end, no matter how controversial or difficult the outcomes.

In that respect Wittgenstein's work here seems closest to that of his fellow Viennese thinker, Sigmund Freud. The person and work of Freud held a lifelong fascination for Wittgenstein, and his sister had in fact undergone a course of psychoanalysis with the Viennese master. Although this was recommended several times to Ludwig, he never himself undertook a course of analysis, preferring, as we have seen, to undergo his own form of harsh philosophical analysis/self-scrutiny in the confines of his Norwegian hut. Yet there are more than passing family resemblances between the methods of the two Viennese masters.[82]

Wittgenstein's remarks about Freud are scattered throughout the *Nachlass*, especially the collection of remarks published as *Culture and Value* and the conversations with Rhees in 1942 published as the *Conversations on Freud* in *Lectures and Conversations on Aesthetics, Psychology and Religious Belief*.[83] In his later thought, Wittgenstein clearly saw the value of Freud's work not as that of a pseudo-scientist but in the function of Freudian analysis as 'aspect-changing':

> When a dream is interpreted we might say that it is fitted into a context in which it ceases to be puzzling. In a sense the dreamer re-dreams his dream in surroundings such that *its aspect changes* ...
>
> In considering what a dream is, it is important to consider what happens to it, the way its aspect changes when it is brought into relation with other things remembered, for instance.[84]

Thus, as we have seen, philosophy, like therapy or counselling, is for Wittgenstein a process of seeing correctly what lies before us – the 'over-look', or *Übersichtlichkeit*, he so frequently mentions. Not for him the endless interpretation of the *psyche*, but rather the calm gaze as we observe its trapped movements. As he put it in the posthumously published *Philosophical Investigations*: 'What is your aim in philosophy? – To show the fly the way out of the fly-bottle.'[85]

As we saw in the previous chapter, this liberation, this healing, was for Wittgenstein achieved not by pure intellectual speculation but by observing the 'foundations of possible buildings' from the perspective of the 'over-look'. For Wittgenstein this involves a choreography of 'what is said' and 'what is shown'. Thus the therapist, counsellor or confessor must of course pay attention to what is said to them, but perhaps more importantly to what is not said but shown. For in these pastoral situations more insight can often be found in the unspoken than in the spoken.

As he stated in his preface to the *Tractatus*, there is what is presented on the written page and what is unwritten, and often 'this second part is the important one'[86]: 'What *can* be shown, *cannot* be said.'[87] Again, at this point we can usefully rely on the terminology of Freud: this is what he termed the 'transference' and 'counter-transference' between the listener and the speaker.

Wittgenstein's philosophical confessions remind us that at the heart of true knowledge lies the confessional act, springing from the same place from which we began this book: our unease and desire to know ourselves. Yet perhaps it is misleading to see Wittgenstein as advocating a type of philosophy that transcends rationality and seeks simply to live in the realm of the *mythos* – no matter how attractive that became for him after the traumas of the Great War.[88] For philosophy, as well as confession embedded within it, has nevertheless a specific and defined logical and grammatical purpose for the practitioner that Wittgenstein was never happy to abdicate.

2. The linguistic power of confession: the return to the everyday
One of the first writers to emphasize the 'therapeutic' within Wittgenstein's writing was Stanley Cavell.[89] By the time Alice Crary's collection *The New Wittgenstein*[90] came out in 2000 it seemed as though the notion had influenced a whole generation of Wittgensteinian scholars. This emphasized the shift in recent Wittgensteinian scholarship away from the understanding of his work as largely *theoretical* (or, in Rorty's words, largely concerned with the reactions and concerns of fellow 'professional philosophers') to an understanding which is built around

seeing his work as contributing to individual existential development, or, as Hosseini describes it in a recent work, 'the development of wisdom'.[91] For Crary this 'therapeutic aim' is largely about helping us to see the 'sources of philosophical confusion' we hold. Thus, for Cavell, the aim of Wittgenstein's philosophy is to bring us back from metaphysical speculation to the everyday discourse of 'forms of life' (*Lebensformen*) where language has its natural home.

In the case of Wittgenstein, I have argued in this chapter, by applying his own search for the *Sprachspiel*/'language-game' to his own writings, the move is from the disembodied Cartesian 'I' to the embodied self of the final philosophy.[92] In this respect Wittgenstein has occasionally been misinterpreted by his commentators. Some of this seems to stem from a fear of engaging with the notion of Wittgenstein as an embodied being – both humanly and sexually. Thus for the later Wittgenstein the end of all philosophical speculation becomes *action*. As he wrote in his notebook of 1946, five years before his death:

> One of the things Christianity says amongst others, I believe, is that all sound doctrines are useless. You have to change your *life* (or the *direction* of your life).
>
> It says that all wisdom is cold; and that you can no more use it for sorting out your life than you can forge iron when it is *cold*.
>
> The point is that good teaching need not necessarily *grab* you; you can follow it as you would a doctor's prescription. – But here you need something to grab you and turn you round – (i.e. this is how I understand it).

Once you have been turned round, you must *stay* turned round.

Wisdom is passionless. But faith by contrast is what Kierkegaard calls a *passion*.[93]

This is the *Umsteigung*, the conversion or *metanoia* that we encountered at the beginning of the Gospels in Chapter One and which Ludwig clearly experienced in Norway in the late 1930s and on the Eastern Front during the Great War. Yet the temptations we have to purge by means of confession are not just existential ones but also logical ones, hence the notion that all philosophy begins with a confession. As he states in his Norway diary on 8 February 1937:

When you are tempted to make general metaphysical statements, ask yourself (always): What cases am I actually thinking of? – What sort of case, what idea, occurs to me? (*welche Vorstellung schwebt mir denn da vor?*). Now something in us resists this question for we seem to jeopardize the ideal through it.[94]

Thus as well as having to fight against general ethical and moral dangers the philosopher-confessor must also fight against a metaphysical temptation – to over-generalize, to create the 'sublime conception' (*die sublime Auffassung*) that will move us from 'concrete cases' to the 'ethereal regions' where 'real signs' replace what we can see in front of our eyes.[95] This notion of the temptation of speech and thought leading us from the reality before us to the 'thin ice' or what he referred to as a "'bluish haze surrounding things" and giving them an interesting appearance'[96] becomes a cornerstone of the later philosophy. The *Investigations* devotes several passages to the idea and it is fundamental for the argument of that work from the first pages onwards:

> The more narrowly we examine actual language, the sharper becomes the conflict between it and our requirement. (For the crystalline purity of logic was, of course, not a *result of investigation:* it was a requirement.) The conflict becomes intolerable; the requirement is now in danger of becoming empty. – We have got on to slippery ice where there is no friction and so in a certain sense the conditions are ideal, but also, just because of that, we are unable to walk.[97]

So the philosopher likewise casts off the temptation to launch out into an ideal language, staying with the actual reality of language before her – something he suggests is simpler and humbler, more in keeping with the hard-won normality and 'ordinary life' of the later embodied man:

> We are under the illusion that what is peculiar, profound, essential, in our investigation, resides in its trying to grasp the incomparable essence of language. That is, the order existing between the concepts of proposition, word, proof, truth, experience, and so on. This order is a *super-order* between – so to speak – *super-concepts*. Whereas, of course, if the words 'language', 'experience', 'world', have a use, it must be as humble a one as that of the words 'table', 'lamp', 'door'.[98]

Such a new life, an embodied life, requires, as he says in his notebook of 4 February 1937, 'new language games'. The mind plays tricks on us and in the illusion of seeking after general fantasies we lose the ability to live life: 'first one must live' he writes on 1 March, 'and then one can philosophize'. Thus the aim of philosophy, especially academic philosophy, is not just to become 'a cleverer person' it is to change the character of the philosopher. 'What is the use of studying philosophy,' as Wittgenstein chided his friend Norman Malcolm after the latter made a trite comment about 'the British national character', 'if all that it does for you is to enable you to talk with some plausibility about some abstruse questions of logic, etc. and if it does not improve your thinking about the important questions of everyday life.'[99] In the same letter, seven years after his Norway experience, he still links true philosophy with true confession, in fact suggesting that confession can be the way of protecting philosophy (and no doubt philosophers) from the intellectual pride and arrogance to which he had once been prey: 'it is, if possible, still more difficult to think, or try to think, really honestly about your life and other people's lives. And the trouble is that thinking about these things is *not thrilling*, but often downright nasty. And when it's nasty then it is *most* important.' It took Malcolm some time to recover from Wittgenstein's anger here but it is plausible to suggest that in this one ill-thought casual remark of Malcolm the older Austrian saw something of his own unreformed character as a young man, with all his prejudices and arrogances, and their consequent temptations.

As Monk points out, and as is well depicted in Derek Jarman's film *Wittgenstein*, Wittgenstein's life encapsulated a slow (and often painful) process of embodiment; unsure of his own sexuality, latterly he was able to sustain physical relationships with others. From the later writings the *embodiment* of his discourse becomes clearer: 'the delightful difference of temperature of the parts of a human body',[100] and in the letter to Drury: 'the thing now is to live in the world in which you are, not to think or dream about the world you would like to be in. Look at people's sufferings, physical and mental, you have them close at hand, and this ought to be a good remedy for your troubles.'[101]

This embodiment accompanies a desire to distract our attention from the search for 'occult entities' that 'occupy our heads'; from concern with the 'purely mental', Wittgenstein wants us to touch, smell, taste, see and hear. All our senses are activated as we encounter his texts. Wittgenstein's prerogative is to demonstrate how the art of 'saying and showing' reveals the essence of human communication. Rather than a sideshow, confession for Wittgenstein becomes the essence of what it is to be a human being – a *homo empathicus*.

3. The transformative power of confession – a linguistic strategy or a window on to the transcendent?
The philosophical encounters of Wittgenstein's confessions, especially his return to embodiment and the call of the everyday, should, however, not blind us to his efforts to place his confessional struggles within a transcendent framework. Time and again throughout his diaries, beginning with the earliest notes from the first decade of the twentieth century, occupying his thoughts in the 1930s

and right up to his final jottings in Ireland and Cambridge before his death, he struggled with the notion of God and the transcendent framework to his philosophy. As he famously remarked to his friend Maurice Drury: 'I am not a religious man but I cannot help seeing every problem from a religious point of view.'[102] The curious ambiguity of the phrase, with its rejection of 'religion' but appreciation of a 'religious point of view', seems to embody much of what the 'religious' meant to Wittgenstein. Since his death, and in the vast ocean of commentary and criticism that has emerged since then, there have been attempts to co-opt him as a closet atheist, or at least a verificationist, or, on the other hand, as an avowed and practising Christian. Neither attempt has been wholly successful and his unique blend of so many strands of nineteenth- and twentieth-century thought – idealism, logical positivism, existentialism, psychologism and linguistics – stubbornly defies simple categorization. Yet, as we review Wittgenstein's struggle to confess, I would argue that it is precisely *this* ambiguity and *difficulty* within Wittgenstein's thought that makes it so helpful in investigating 'the religious point of view' in the contemporary world. As we move slowly into a post-Christian world where faith struggles to be defined in a 'secular age', Wittgenstein's own struggles to articulate the 'religious point of view' seem increasingly relevant.

When researching his biography of the philosopher, Ray Monk approached the Catholic priest Fr Conrad Pepler, OP, who had heard Wittgenstein's confession and given him the last rites shortly before he died in Cambridge in April 1951. Questioned by Monk as to the nature of Wittgenstein's beliefs, Pepler replied:

> My lasting impression is that we talked about God in general terms and not about Catholic 'doctrines' nor his relationship to the Church. I certainly came away from the talks with the impression that he was seeking God, to know God. As a result I personally of course am sure that Wittgenstein is with God now – indeed he may never have been far from him.[103]

Although some commentators have suggested that Wittgenstein had no interest in 'the God question', what Pepler describes as his constant search for God is very apparent from a glance at the unpublished notebooks that we have been discussing in this chapter. When the 'Secret Notebook' appeared in 1985 its editor, Baum, remarked that it showed the 'Christian Form of Life with religion as one of the chief matrices for understanding his work',[104] and acquaintances such as Engelmann, from whom we have quoted throughout this chapter, were in no doubt that the transcendent perspective was essential to understanding Wittgenstein's theory of meaning. As he wrote in his recollections of his conversations with Wittgenstein:

> A whole generation of disciples was able to take Wittgenstein for a positivist because he has something of enormous importance in common with the positivists: he draws the line between what we can speak about and what we must be silent about just as they do. The difference is only that they have nothing to be

silent about. Positivism holds – and this is its essence – that what we can speak about is all that matters in life. *Whereas Wittgenstein passionately believes that all that really matters in human life is precisely what, in his view, we must be silent about.* When he nevertheless takes immense pains to delimit the unimportant, it is not the coastline of that island which he is bent on surveying with such meticulous accuracy, but the boundary of the ocean.[105]

One of the consequences of the publication of Wittgenstein's confessions is that we can now appreciate anew how much this struggle with the transcendent meant for Wittgenstein throughout his life and how much these struggles were intertwined with the articulation and interpretation of his philosophy. Even in his First World War notebooks at the beginning of his writing career he juxtaposes observations on logical grammar with deep and personal appeals to the Almighty. Seen from this perspective, the 'pure' philosophizing of the *Tractatus* seems to have arisen from a distinctively embodied context, one that includes *Glaubensfragen*/questions of faith, prayers and entreaties to God. 'Now comes inspection. My soul shrivels up. God give me light! God give me light! God give light to my soul!' he writes in the crucial year of 1916.[106] Adding a day later:

Do your best. You cannot do more: and be cheerful ... Help yourself and help others with all your strength. And at the same time be cheerful! But how much strength should one need for oneself and how much for others? It is hard to live well!! But it is good to live well. However, not mine, but Thy will be done.[107]

The fervent and passionate quality of his entries was no doubt intertwined with the Tolstovian revelations we mentioned earlier. Thus we find him writing on 8 December 1914:

> Christianity is indeed the only sure way to happiness but what if someone spurned that happiness?! Might it not be better to perish unhappily in the hopeless struggle against the external world? But such a life is senseless. But why not lead a senseless life? Is it unworthy?[108]

Twenty years later, writing in his Norwegian hut, his struggles to get to grips with the Gospels continued. As he battled with despair and depression in the long Norwegian winter he set about reading the Bible, wondering whether his belief should be based on 'nothing but a document' or on his own 'enlightenment' (*einleuchten*) – 'only conscience can command me – to believe in resurrection, judgement etc.'[109] – for 'one must begin with belief … from words no belief follows'. The old Tolstovian fideism remained, but now Wittgenstein tempered his struggle with other insights. Might the struggle, he suggests, lead him to 'cast oneself into the arms of grace'?[110] He may well 'reject the Christian solution of the problem of life', he wrote on 4 February[111] but 'this does not solve the problem of my life … I am not saved'. Yet his thought returns again and again to the Scriptures as he works through his issues of conscience: 'as the insect buzzes around the light, so I buzz around the New Testament'.[112] Followed by a direct entreaty to the Almighty: 'God! Help me come into a relationship with you in which I can be happy with my work. I believe that at every moment God can demand <u>everything</u> from you! Is really conscious of you! So I ask that he gives you the gift of life!'[113] For, as he admits on 13 February: 'Whatever may be true or false in regard to the New Testament, one thing cannot be doubted: that in order to live <u>right</u> I would have to live completely differently from what suits me.'[114]

The call to change one's life, to confess all, thus comes from the belief that 'at every moment God can demand <u>everything</u> from you! ... So I ask that he gives you the gift of life!' Throughout the diaries we find Wittgenstein 'treading on the thin ice across deep water'[115] as he vacillates between the desire to believe in God and his buzzing around the Scriptures and his self-recognition of the trouble he has professing himself a believer.[116] Yet it is precisely from this ambiguous desire for the transcendent that Wittgenstein's 'philosophical confessions' arise: encapsulating not just the desire for confession but also the new formulation of his later philosophy with its confessional style that prods and provokes the reader. As he says shortly after the previous diary entry: '<u>Don't explain!</u> – <u>Describe!</u>' / '<u>Nicht erklären! Beschreiben!</u>' A clear echo of the famous injunction from the *Philosophical Investigations*: 'Don't think – Look!'

Yes, we can argue, Wittgenstein *was* a believer – but what sort of believer? In the diaries he describes himself as one who kneels for prayer and then suddenly says 'there is no-one here',[117] which somehow makes him feel relieved. In this loneliness, in this praying that isn't praying, Wittgenstein, through his confessional philosophy, finds what he has been searching for ('I thank God that I have come to Norway into the loneliness!').[118] 'This is no Christianity' he admits, for:

> This striving for the absolute which makes all worldly happiness appear too petty, which turns our gaze upward and not <u>level</u>, towards the things, appears as something glorious, sublime to me; but I <u>myself</u> turn my gaze towards worldly things, unless 'God visits me'.[119]

For, as he points out, he makes a distinction between 'the actual Christian faith' (*eigentlich Christenglauben*) and 'belief' (*Glauben*).[120] This 'belief' – the glance to the transcendent – is the origin of his desire to confess, yet it is not a belief that will lead him to organized Christian faith as such:

> I don't have a belief in a salvation through the death of Christ; or at least not yet. I also don't feel that I am on the way to such a belief, but I consider it possible that one day I will understand something here of which I understand nothing now.

As he writes on 15 February: 'For what can be said by way of a simile, that can also be said without a simile (*Gleichnis*).[121] … All I could really do is make a gesture (*Geste*) which means something similar to "unsayable" (*unsagbar*) and say nothing.'[122] The position, surely, of the end of the earlier *Tractatus*: 'Of what we cannot speak, we must pass over in silence.'[123]

Yet, the middle-aged Wittgenstein tempers the apophaticism of the young man: 'or is this absolute aversion to using words here some sort of flight? A flight from reality?' But, as before, the ambiguity remains (and notice again Wittgenstein's propensity to have conversations with himself, taken over into the published remarks of the *Investigations*): 'I don't think so; but I don't know.' He concludes the entry in secret code: 'Let me not shy away from any conclusion, but absolutely also not be superstitious!! <u>I do not want to think uncleanly!</u> God! Let me come into a relation to you in which I "can be cheerful in my work".' As stated before, the very ambiguity of his remarks and working methods swings open the doors of the soul on to the confessional.

Thus Wittgenstein in his confessional philosophy opens the door to the transcendent (or, as he calls it, 'the abyss of the human heart'), gazes at it, but does not step through that door. As he sat in his dark hermitage in Norway formulating a new style of philosophy that would have such an impact on a post-religious world he realized that he himself must 'heal his soul', for:

> Faith is faith in what is needed by my *heart*, my *soul*, not my speculative intelligence. For it is my soul with its passions, as it were with its flesh and blood, that has to be saved, not my abstract mind. Perhaps we can say: only *love* can believe the Resurrection. Or, it is *love* that believes the Resurrection.[124]

Like Lord Tristan, whom we left on his sick-bed in the previous chapter, Wittgenstein gazes into the abyss and realizes a way forward for the troubled postmodern soul. In his case strengthened and renewed through the purifying power of confession – a power that enables him to open the door on to the healing possibility of the transcendent.

'In my soul now it is winter ... everything is snowed in', he wrote in his Norwegian hut in February 1937.[125] But one day, he hoped, everything might turn green and blossom: 'I should therefore patiently await to see whether I am destined to see a spring.' Let us hope, with Conrad Pepler, that Ludwig Wittgenstein, the troubled religious genius of the twentieth century, did eventually witness that spring in his soul.

CHAPTER FOUR

GOD'S LAUGHTER:
THE CONFESSIONS OF
SWAMI ABHISHIKTANANDA

His eyes twinkled. That struck me immediately. His bright, sparkling gaze. And the comical nimbus of white hair. A jester in the court of God, I realized him to be, then, in that first impression, with his disorganized simplicity ...

At the mouth of the *guha* (cave) Swamiji did know mirth. The encounter deep within the speechless silence of himself did not eclipse or deflate the garrulous human reality where, doggedly less than absolute, we pursue our foolish way. Swamiji knew that paradox, the comical disproportion between *advaitic* experience and the ordinary, daily world.[1]

The late-middle-aged Breton Henri Le Saux, later and better known as Swami Abhishiktananda, certainly made a lasting impression on all who met him in India during his final years in the late 1960s and early 1970s.[2] An emaciated and very white Frenchman, he had for the past twenty years worn the *kavi* – the saffron robe of the Hindu *sannyāsi* – the one who renounces all worldly ties and seeks only the Beyond, living a life of complete poverty and always carrying the all-important begging bowl. Yet, the 'clown of God', this slightly alarming and amusing figure, was also a highly trained Catholic priest and theologian. With his fellow would-be ascetic Fr Jules Monchanin, he had struggled for most of his adult life to reconcile the demands of the lifestyle of the Indian ascetic with those of his Catholic inheritance and position.

Half a century after his death in 1973 the problems and issues that beset him during his relatively short time in India stay with us and if anything have become even more relevant in a world rent by sectarian violence and religious extremism. Le Saux's dilemma: how can I be true to my origins while reaching out and befriending the 'other' through new encounters in the contemporary world – in particular the 'other' in religious and cultural terms – remains our dilemma too. In this respect Swamiji was a pioneer ahead of his time.[3] In his final years he would often encounter the youth of Europe, disenchanted and led to India by the material desert of the West, many of whom recognized him as the 'original hippie' – an epithet he became rather fond of. Yet the weird hipster was also a serious and erudite spiritual seeker. The testimony to this is held in three sources. First, there are the accounts of the Swami by writers such as Kenneth Sharpe, with whom we began. Second, there are his numerous writings to a vast and multifaceted public, in particular his books and his letters. The former were published at intervals throughout his life, mostly in French and English, and were usually later derided by the Swami, who grew out of their opinions almost as soon as they were written, becoming increasingly convinced that what he was seeking could not be articulated in traditional prose and discourse. Ultimately he expressed satisfaction only with the more autobiographical accounts of his encounters with various Indian mystics and sages such as Srī Ramana Maharshi and Srī Gnānānanda. Finally, there is his 'confession' – his spiritual diary which he kept assiduously from the first stirrings of his encounter with the Indian other to the final flowering in his extraordinary and remarkable *mahāprasthāna*, his 'great departure' to the other side. As with our readings of Wittgenstein, it is in the fire of Swamiji's confession that we enter into the crucible in which Swamiji's faith was forged. As with many of the personal confessions and utterances explored in this book, we also have to ask ourselves: *should* we be reading them? Were they meant for us to read? How far can we use them to draw conclusions about the nature of the beliefs of those who wrote them? As Raimundo Panikkar, who edited the diaries, concurs: 'This diary was not written with a view to publication ... Is this not highly indiscreet, a kind of profanation of what, out of respect for the experience of a spiritual man, ought to remain hidden?'[4]

And in fact the first editor of his diary, his follower Marc Chaduc, seemingly took the liberty (rather like Anscombe editing Wittgenstein's diary) of removing many of the personal references in the later parts of the text. Panikkar, on the contrary, recognized that the personal 'fire' of the diary was indeed part of Swamiji's legacy. For if we simply encounter the pale Breton wandering around rather dazed in late-1960s hippie India, or read the theological treatises that he left us, we shall probably miss the main event – the personal encounter in what he loved to call 'the cave of the heart'.[5] For, as Panikkar states, the text of the diary:

> gushes up from the author's being, as he lets his pen run freely. This diary is, so to speak, the laboratory of an alchemist; the forerunner of something unknown. The author is feeling his way, searching for himself, following endless meanders as experience at every level invades his life.[6]

As with all the personal texts we have encountered in this book, we have, then, to approach the diary of Swamiji with a particular hermeneutic, for we are dealing as much with affairs of the heart as with affairs of the head. As with so many of the personalities we have explored in this volume, *cor ad cor loquitur* – we speak beyond the head into the heart. And as we watch the spiritual transformation of a fellow human being, often through great struggle and darkness, we can begin to appreciate our own dark struggles confronted with the Beyond. In addition, in the case of Swamiji we have the privilege of watching the struggles of a pioneer, like a mountaineer or polar explorer, taking one faltering step after another as they slowly and laboriously forge a path never before taken. Augmented with that glorious and precise tool, hindsight, we can see where the pioneer made mistakes and from which we can learn for our own journeys. Swamiji's case is particularly poignant for, in the words of Panikkar, who himself was a *confidant* of the seeker, in being 'faithful to the truth he was overwhelmed by it'.[7] For, if nothing else, a reading of Swamiji's confessions shows us again the truth of

Kierkegaard's *dictum* that so moved Wittgenstein: faith alone must be a passion. In this respect he calls us again to that *metanoia*, the change of heart, that our troubled times demand. As Panikkar states in the preface to the diary: 'Humanity in these days can only be saved if it is capable of a profound conversion – all human culture today is in need of a radical *metanoia* – without becoming the victim of a destructive alienation.'[8]

For Swamiji's struggle, no less than that of his great forebear Gandhi, was that between modern globalized technocratic (and late-capitalist) humanity and the pre-modern humanity represented to him by the *sadhus* and *swamis* he encountered in modern India. In tracing that struggle we shall, as we have done throughout this book, draw out the implications, spiritual and psychological, for the spiritual seeker today.

THE HINDU–CHRISTIAN ENCOUNTER

There is no doubt that the young Père Henri, fresh from France, was keen to follow in the footsteps of his missionary forebears and convert Hindus to Christianity. As he wrote in an early entry in his diary on 31 March 1952, he saw Hinduism and Christianity as two distinct religions, of which Christianity was definitive, and he was sure that eventually 'Hinduism will merge into Christianity'.[9] This he came to refer to later as his 'fulfillment' view of the relation between the two ancient faiths: 'It is a matter of incorporating into my Christianity all the positive values of Hinduism, thought, worship, devotion, while rejecting only what is clearly and surely incompatible, and of re-interpreting in Christian terms whatever cannot enter just as it is.'[10]

For the deeply intellectual and sophisticated Le Saux and Monchanin this would revolve around the appropriation of the ancient Hindu traditions of prayer, meditation and renunciation and a deep and introspective study of the Sanskrit Scriptures, especially the *Vedas* and *Upanishads*. In addition, during these early days at Shantivanam (and never dropped by Fr Monchanin), there was the emphasis on the incorporation into Christian *praxis* of anything which was considered compatible from the Indian tradition while leaving aside that which was considered unacceptable. Le Saux wrote to his father back in France on 16 September 1948:

> [The Hindus] cannot understand that it is obligatory to have a definite faith, a fixed creed, and to belong to the Church. The nearer I come to these Hindus, the more I feel them at the same time close to me in their loyal search for God, and far from me in their psychological inability to admit that Christianity is the only authentic means of coming to God.[11]

This was all destined to change for Le Saux a year later as he had his first fateful encounter with the ageing Hindu seer Ramana Maharshi in 1949. Born in 1879 in simple circumstances in Tiruchuzhi in Tamil Nadu, Ramana had first received his experience of *advaita*, or 'non-duality', at the age of seventeen[12] while having to deal with a violent fear of death.[13] He was left with the fundamental question, 'Who am I, really, really?', which he would

get his followers to ask themselves constantly, so stripping self-image until all non-essential conceptions of self
had been removed. Shortly after this realization the seer
had withdrawn to the holy mountain of Arunāchala in
Tamil Nadu, which turned out to be near Le Saux's new
Christian ashram at Shantivanam.[14] Encouraged by their
enlightened bishop, Le Saux and Monchanin paid a visit
to Ramana's ashram in January 1949. Yet, Le Saux's first
encounter with the ageing guru was, he confessed, an
anti-climax:

> I felt let down, and in my disappointment sadness filled
> my heart … Surrounded by this ritual, these prostra-
> tions, the cloud of incense, and the crowd of people
> sitting silently with their eyes fixed on him, this man
> seemed so natural, so 'ordinary', a kindly grandfather,
> shrewd and serene, very like my own, as I remembered
> him from my childhood. I did not know what to make
> of him.[15]

Despite this disappointing first encounter – and taking
into account the young Le Saux's views on Hinduism, such
a negative reaction was probably to be expected – a seed
had been planted within his heart. This, as we shall see,
would become something of a pattern in his life and his
encounter with the 'other': initially his intellect would
place barriers, but meanwhile unconsciously, in 'the
heart', other forces would move slowly and silently, with
later unexpected consequences.

Six months later he returned to Arunāchala only to
discover that Srī Ramana was dying of cancer and all

audiences had been restricted. As he waited for the *darśana* with the Maharshi he learnt more of his message from his followers.[16] He was told that:

> The most central point in Srī Ramana's teaching is the mystery of the heart … Find the heart deep within oneself, beyond mind and thought, make that one's permanent dwelling, cut all the bonds which keep this heart at the level of sense and outward consciousness, all the fleeting identifications of what one *is*, with what one *has* or what one *does*.[17]

He was also given a verse of the *Upanishads* to meditate upon, which would remain central to his search for the rest of his time on earth:

> Heaven is within the inner chamber,
> The glorious place,
> Which is entered by those who renounce themselves![18]

This cave, or *guha*, of the heart would become a constant trope in Swamiji's later writings. As well as the metaphorical cave, Swamiji took this opportunity to acquaint himself with the actual caves of Arunāchala and to 'meditate in the Indian way'.[19] As he would later write in his diary: 'The caves of Arunāchala are the *guha*, Brahman inhabits the *guha* of the heart, as the Upanishads say (e.g. Katha Upanishad 11: 20). Here it is the *guha* of Brahman himself, not so much where he abides in me as where I abide in him.'[20]

The seed of Arunāchala and Ramana would begin to germinate and for the rest of his life Swamiji would not forget these encounters (Ramana himself passed away two years after Swamiji's visits, in 1952). Later he would write in his diary, in conscious reflection of the poems of St John of the Cross, to whom we shall return later, during the silence of his thirty-two days at Mauna Mandir in November 1956:

You have ravished me, O Arunāchala!
Like a young girl to whom someone has made love,
And you have left me here, like this, before you ...
They all stare at me, and they laugh at me ...
O Arunāchala! Since you have ravished me, carry me away,
Or else finish me off!
Since you have wounded me, kill me, or else heal me! ...
Your face brushed against mine, your arms were extended,
And I offered my lips and held out my arms,
And You, You laughed at me, and withdrew it,
Your Mystery,
Beyond my reach![21]

This encounter with Arunāchala and its mystic heart would be, he would later admit, the turning point of his life, especially as to how he regarded the relationship between Hinduism and Christianity. From the pre-Arunāchala days of Christian fulfilment of Hinduism he had been plunged into a dangerous and whirling dance of the two faiths which threatened to capsize him. As he later wrote to Odette Baumer-Despeigne, the editor of his posthumously published *Secret of Arunāchala*:

> The confrontation between Christianity and Vedanta has been at the centre of my life since the caves of Arunāchala. It was first expressed in *Guhantara*, which you did not think much of ... The intuition which was worked out in *Sagesse* came to me towards 1960; but the further I went, the more impossible it became to bear the strain of maintaining this insight (nothing physical or psychological, but rather like a 'count-down' of an extreme tension).[22]

From this time onwards, then, an unbearable tension was established in his life which he could rarely confess to unless in his private diary or to his closest friends in letters and conversations. In 1969 he would write to Anne-Marie Stokes: 'I find it more and more difficult to see how to integrate Christianity with Hindu experience – and yet this is essential for catholicity ... How to carry through the present mutation of Christianity without obscuring its essence?'[23]

And crucial to resolving or at least understanding this tension was Swamiji's attitude to the one he called his '*sad-guru*' – his root guru – Jesus Christ.

WHOM DO YOU SAY THAT I AM?

One of the most challenging aspects of Swamiji's journey, even today, is the development of his understanding of what he constantly referred to as his '*sad-guru*'[24] – that is, his root

or source guru – Jesus Christ. Before the Arunāchala experience his view, as noted above, was more or less that of a
conventional French priest of the mid-twentieth century.
However, the secret encounter of Arunāchala began a
long questioning process that had unexpected results. In
1954 he started to confess to being tormented by 'his two
loves'[25]: Christianity and Hinduism. As he meditated on
the nature of Christ he felt he had two choices: either to
consider Christ 'simply as his chosen symbol to express
the transcendent mystery (*ishtadevatha*)' or to see him as
'simply a manifestation at the level of phenomena (*nāmā
rūpa*)' of the Ultimate Unknowingness. The notion of
Christ as the manifestation in *nāmā rūpa* (in name and
form) of the God beyond concepts was Swamiji's answer
to the challenge of a notion central to the teaching of the
Upanishads – that is, that God is 'not this, not that' – *neti,
neti* – and that any attempt to apply a concept, name or
form to God was mistaken. Thus as late as 1970 he could
write in his diary: 'Jesus is the *sadguru*. By that very fact
he leads beyond his form. He constantly refers to the
Father. He is only the Father's echo.'[26] Refining this a few
months later: 'Jesus is that mystery that "grounds" me, that
"sources" me, in the abyss, in the bottomless *guha* – the
mystery (as we say) of the Father.'[27]

This notion of Christ as the revelation of the 'father' or
begetter, as that beyond forms and unknown to us, was to
have a big impact on one of Swamiji's colleagues and followers whom we have already mentioned, Raimundo Panikkar
(the person who was later to prepare Swamiji's private
diary for publication). In his *The Trinity and the Religious
Experience of Man*, written shortly before Swamiji's death in

1973 while he was a professor in California and described by Archbishop Rowan Williams as 'one of the best and least read meditations on the Trinity in our century',[28] he follows through the implications of Swamiji's position to present a daringly radical and original interpretation of the Christian doctrine of the Trinity. Like Swamiji, he sees the Father as the 'abyss', beyond names, the '*a-nāmā*':

> One can call this Absolute brahman or one can call it tao. But tao, once named, is no longer tao and brahman, if known, is no longer brahman. The God that is seen is no longer the God (*o theós*) for no one has ever seen God; 'no one can see him and live'. His transcendence is constitutive and he alone is authentically transcendent.[29]

From the perspective of the 'unknown Father', Panikkar asks the rhetorical question (no doubt stimulated by his encounter with *advaita*), 'is it possible to conceive a religion based exclusively on our "relation" with the Divinity?'[30] to which his answer is: 'I do not think so, for the simple reason that no relationship is even conceivable with the Absolute as immanent.' But, instead of excluding immanence from the experience of religion, he proposes that 'this dimension of immanence' is the 'horizon from which the God of the "religions" emerges'.[31] This manifest form is for him 'the Son' – Christ. With regard to other religions than Christianity, he states:

> It is not my task to discuss the other names and titles that have been accorded to this manifestation of the Mystery

in other religious traditions. The reason I persist in calling it Christ is that it seems to me that phenomenologically Christ presents the fundamental characteristics of the mediator between divine and cosmic, eternal and temporal, etc., which other religions call *Iśvara*, *Tathāgata*, or even Jahweh, Allah and so on.[32]

Christ thus becomes for Panikkar (at the time of writing *The Trinity and the Religious Experience of Man*) the nexus where this revelation of the immanence of God finds its fullest expression. Therefore, in relation to other religions, Christianity is not claiming that it is '*the* religion for the whole of mankind' but rather that it is the place 'where Christ is fully revealed, the end and plenitude of every religion'.[33] Panikkar's decision to place the fullness of revelation in the Christian Church (in 1973 at least) contrasts with Swamiji's discomfort, certainly as expressed in his private diaries. And, as we earlier quoted Panikkar as having written, there is perhaps a sense of unease in drawing out the private musings of a man in conflict into the clear light of day: 'is this not highly indiscreet, a kind of profanation of what, out of respect for the experience of a spiritual man, ought to remain hidden?'[34] Yet, as has often been stated in this book, one of the key aspects of confession is the ultimate dilemma – what should be revealed and what hidden. In confession there is a necessary draw to reveal all, to pose the unanswerable and the unbearable, and this is exactly what Swamiji does in 1969, having received one of the early articles Panikkar was working on as he moved towards the theology presented in his 1973 book on the Trinity.[35]

In a letter addressed to his old friend, Swamiji reveals how, like Walt Whitman, he will 'sail forth and steer for the deep waters only, for we are bound where mariner has not yet dared to go, and we will risk the ship, ourselves and all'. From his late *advaitan* perspective Swamiji suggests that 'Christ shares the transitoriness of the world of manifestation, of *maya*. Finally he disappears.'[36] Thus, Christ 'may be useful for awakening the soul', like any guru, but 'is never essential, and, like the guru, he himself must in the end lose all his personal characteristics', for 'no one really needs him': 'whoever, in his personal experience ... has discovered the Self, has no need of faith in Christ, of prayer, of the communion of the Church'. This is strong stuff and suggests why Swamiji suffered so much for so many long years after his Arunāchala encounter all those years before. If this really had been the nature of the revelation of Arunāchala, no wonder it had blown a hole through his preconceptions of Christ and the Church and led him to the dark cave of the confessional diary. In a later letter to Sr Sara Grant he reiterated the theme, emphasizing the relative 'unimportance' of Christ from an *advaitan* perspective:

> Why then call him only Jesus of Nazareth? Why say that it is Jesus of Nazareth whom others unknowingly call Shiva or Krishna? And not rather say that Jesus is the theophany for *us*, Bible-believers, of that unnameable mystery of the Manifestation, always tending beyond itself, since Brahman transcends all its/his manifestations.[37]

Swamiji's dilemma was never to be resolved for him by means of theology. On the one hand the manifestation of

Christ as the immanent in the realm of *nāmā rūpa* placed him on a par with other manifestations such as Shiva or Krishna, whereas the desire to avoid this (as Panikkar and later theologians such as Williams and D'Costa do) by stressing the unique nature of Christ means for Swamiji that Christianity loses its catholicity.[38] 'I do not see', he concluded in his 1969 letter to Panikkar, 'how one can escape from this dilemma.'

In a fascinating thesis, John Friesen argues that Abhishiktananda develops a view that is beyond *advaita* and *non-advaita*.[39] In the Diary entry of 3 April 1952[40] the Swami states that Jesus' statement that 'the Father and I are one' 'should be regarded at the same time as in *dvaita* and *advaita*'.[41] Jesus, Friesen suggests, 'addresses God as the "Other" but at the same time Jesus acts like God'. Friesen's suggestion that Swamiji presents a 'non-monistic *advaita*', no doubt fertilized by his conversations with Panikkar on the Trinity in the 1960s, whereby Christ stands for *advaita* and duality in respect to the 'Father' held together by the 'non-duality' of the Spirit,[42] presents an interpretation that would, I am sure, have appealed to Abhishiktananda himself.[43] In Indian philosophical tradition *dvaita* and *advaita* are conceptually opposed, and towards the end of his life Abhishiktananda seemed to recognize the theological shipwreck his reasoning had undergone on these nasty theological reefs. As he wrote to Odette Baumer-Despeigne on 5 December 1970, shortly before his death:

In *Sagesse* I attempted a meditative approach within the framework of classical theology. The last chapter shows that the problem is unresolved. The best course is still,

I think, to hold on under extreme tension to the two forms of unique 'faith' until the dawn appears. For *advaita* and theology are on two levels.[44]

In his final years he seems to have had less and less time for theology as traditionally practised, as he developed a new *praxis* for living the Christian life in the modern world. As he wrote in his last diary entry on 12 September 1973:

The Trinity can only be understood in the experience of *advaita*. The Trinity is an experience, not a *theologoumenon* (theological formulation) ... The Trinity is the ultimate mystery of oneself. But in the very depth of this discovery of the Self-Trinity there lies the paradox: in the mystery of the non-source, who still speaks of the Source?

At this point in his journey, rather like for Wittgenstein, language itself begins to break down in the hands of the Swami, leading to the final statement in his diary: 'The non-awakening, the not-born, is manifested by a – what? – a brilliance, a light, a glory that envelops everything, that transcends everything, that seizes one and takes one beyond everything. A sense of "Beyond", of the Beyond ...'[45] It is as though the final stage of confession, as for Wittgenstein, becomes the inexorable passage into silence itself.

ABHISHIKTANANDA'S WAY

Abhishiktananda and his fellow monks epitomize a dilemma that lies at the heart of religion. On the one hand, the need to codify and direct its manifestations into the

channels of civilized life; on the other, the wild frontiers
of the experience which, in a way, can never be tamed. In
later life, as he encountered the *rishis* and *sadhus* of old
India on the banks of the Ganges with their wild dread-
locks and crazy ways, he felt he was encountering once
again the original, and dangerous, face of religion. As he
wrote to his protégé, the Carmelite sister Thérèse de Jésus
(Lemoine) in 1969: 'Remember the hermits of Blessed
Albert. The Church needs that witness, which cannot be
codified and institutionalized. The deep reason for the
present crisis is the exaltation of human laws above the
Lord and of theology above experience of God.'[46]

We shall return to 'the hermits of Blessed Albert' in
the following chapter. For now it is worth mapping out
the implications for us of Abhishiktananda's reflections on
this lived experience of religion as directed away from its
theological evaluation. At its heart, for the Swami, it is a
move away from the Western codification of ideas *about*
God towards the encounter with the living mystery of
God – the *metanoia*, turning or repentance that Christ had
proclaimed at the beginning of his ministry. At root this
turning, for Swamiji, lay at the centre of the modern crisis
of faith and religion (and in the present book becomes the
primordial act of the confessional turn). As he put it to
Odette Baumer-Despeigne towards the end of his life as
he lived as a solitary hermit by the banks of the Ganges at
Gyansu in Uttar Pradesh:

> To write? To write? What is most true cannot be writ-
> ten, as I have just found by experience at the Phulchatti
> ashram. When the time comes the Spirit will dictate

what should be said. To express that 'beyond', theology is no longer sufficient; it requires poetry or its
equivalent.[47]

The cosmos certainly conspired to reinforce his new-found
resolution when his expensive French typewriter was
shortly thereafter stolen from his hermitage – he was never
able to use it again. From this time onwards the awareness
of what he termed 'I AM' replaced all 'christo-logy'.[48] The
fatal turn in Christianity had been, he considered, its infec-
tion by the Greek ideal of conceptualization at the expense
of experience:

> The Gospel does not exist to teach *ideas*, but to confront
> each one's attitude in face of the mystery with that of
> Jesus. That is existential and real. It is the Greeks who
> have turned the Gospel into a *gnosis*. By means of India's
> *jñana* we must throw out this gnosis and rediscover the
> freshness of the experience of Jesus, freeing ourselves
> in the process also from our Vedantin formulations –
> which are just as limiting as those of the Jews and
> Greeks.[49]

His dissatisfaction with Christianity was such that he could
confide in his diary in 1955: 'I no longer find any consola-
tion in the Church, not even any help. I keep up the cult out
of duty and so recite the formulas I am bound to recite.'[50]
Yet as he lost his identification with traditional Christianity
after his Arunāchala experience he still felt alienated from
the Hindu world. As he wrote in 1955: 'Dislocation. Too
Hindu to form Christian monks, too Christian to be totally

at ease in Hinduism.'[51] The dislocation at this time in the
mid-1950s became so extreme he even felt that he could
no longer go on living:

> I can no longer live as a Christian monk here; and I
> cannot live as a Hindu monk. May the Lord take pity
> on me and cut short my life! I cannot take any more.[52]

> I often dream of dying, for it seems there is no way
> out for me in this life. I cannot be at the same time
> both Hindu and Christian, and no more can I be either
> simply Hindu or simply Christian. So what is the point
> of living? How little heart it leaves me for living.[53]

Yet out of this fierce cauldron, torn, as he wrote, 'between
Arunāchala and Rome',[54] he was ultimately able to forge a
new way based, as we have seen, not on theology (which at
this stage in his journey he found largely unhelpful), but on
his experience of God, especially as conveyed in meditation and prayer. In his later years he would describe himself
as a 'bridge' between *advaita* and Christianity, even if, like
all bridges, he would have to take the strain of maintaining
the tension between the two. Even though his mind, as we
have seen, sought an intellectual resolution of the quandary
he felt himself in, his heart was slowly drawn to live with
the 'bridge' experience and the necessary, and hopefully
creative, tension that it brought. As he wrote in 1967: 'We
have to accept ourselves as the Lord made us. I can neither
have a brown skin nor speak an Indian mother-tongue.
Instead of lamenting the fact, each has to infer from it
where his own vocation lies.'[55] This 'bridging vocation'
would, he suggested, communicate 'the Hindu message

to Christianity and the Christian message to Hindus'.[56] How then could this 'bridging vocation' be accomplished? What, in the final reckoning, was Abhishiktananda's way?

James Stuart, in his review of Swamiji's last books, suggests that at this stage in his life Abhishiktananda had three tasks to perform.[57] First, to share with others, especially non-Indians, the spirituality of India, in particular *advaita*. Second, a form of '*ressourcement*' – the call popular from the 1950s onwards for Christians to return to their spiritual roots which, Stuart argues, was his response to the late-twentieth-century spiritual crisis of the West – no doubt magnified by his encounters with the spiritually hungry, but lost, young hippies he met on the banks of the Ganges during his final years. Finally, Stuart suggests, he was trying to work towards a 'theological integration' of Hindu and Christian experience. Yet, as argued above and as Stuart himself admits, this final aim was abandoned not long after his book, *Sagesse*, was published, no doubt for the reasons we have just outlined.[58] The final path of Abhishiktananda, once he had completed his theological struggles with his dilemma, would end up being much simpler. Rather, we can see the last years of his quest as being dominated by a triad which he himself repeatedly mentions: silence, solitude and poverty.[59]

As a Benedictine monk, Abhishiktananda had always valued 'the sound of silence' and it had long been incorporated into his daily routine. Not, of course, the silence of 'keeping the mouth closed' but rather the cultivation of a silence of the spirit. Drawing on the tradition of the desert elders whom we encountered earlier in this book and who were the original inspiration for St Benedict, the contemporary writer John Chryssavgis describes this monastic silence as:

> a way of waiting, a way of watching and a way of listening ... it is a way of interiority, of stopping and then of exploring the cellars of the heart and the centre of life ... Silence is never merely a cessation of words ... rather it is the pause that holds together all the words both spoken and unspoken. Silence is the glue that connects our attitudes and actions. It is fullness not emptiness, it is not an absence but the awareness of a presence.[60]

Such a silence had always been part of Swamiji's life, but in 1956, partly inspired by the meeting with his second Hindu guru, Srī Gnānānanda, earlier that year, he spent five weeks in total silence at Mauna Mandir ('The Temple of Silence') at Kumbakonam. Such was the level of the isolation, he did not even see the face of the person who brought his food every day, only their hands as they placed it on the turnstile. The experience had a profound impact on him as outlined in his private diary. Such was its power that when the door was finally opened at the end and he met his helpers he burst into tears. Later, in a letter to the Millers in 1970, he felt that the 'real solution' to the situation in which he found himself, poised between *advaita* and Christianity, was 'to learn the language of silence', even if he admitted he was 'too Greek to be able to free myself from speculation, even though everything around invites me to do so'.[61] The admission of his 'Greek failure' is touching, as though as his pilgrimage came to an end he had begun to accept his vocation 'as the Lord had made him'. Thus Abhishiktananda's silence becomes an attempt 'to sensitize people to the questioning by the Spirit through India, in an effort to awaken the Christians'.[62] His was indeed a *ressourcement*, as Stuart suggests, but a *ressourcement* to the springs of Christian mystical theology where the name of the Father is unspoken and unknown and which we shall return to in the following chapter. It was a *ressourcement* to the heart. Faith, in this respect, becomes 'simply the acceptance that there is something beyond the rational'.[63] Wittgenstein had opened the door to the transcendent. Abhishiktananda had taken the next step through the doors and encountered the abyss of silence that lay there. For him, beyond all religions and perhaps beyond all human experience, this was transformed into the power of his confession.

As his fame spread, the demand to give talks and present this new 'Christian *advaita*', especially in the West, grew stronger. Once again we cannot but admire the honesty and integrity of the man as he forensically examined the various facets of this new and somewhat surprising turn at the end of his life in the confession of his diary.

Swami Abhishiktananda lived at the dawn of our modern age of gurus, self-help manuals and Eastern spiritual enchantment evidenced by the throngs of young seekers on their way to Rishikesh in the wake of the Beatles. His desire for solitude away from this spiritual circus impresses even today, as does his forensic examination of the pathology that lies at the heart of this whirligig:

They say that 'yoga' (what do they mean by that?) is spreading more and more – yoga groups conducted by

swamis which are now leading Christians astray from
their faith. 'Christian yoga groups' (they say) which
have fully made their own the Vedantin experience
are needed to counterbalance the influence ... I have
grave doubts about the depth of all this. They want a
Vedanta adapted for westerners, the sort of thing that is
freely dispensed by the swami commercial-travellers in
Vedanta ... the monk is not called to go running around
the world.[64]

For him the call was to be a monk, not 'a salesman of solitude and monastic life'.[65] Once again he was resisting,
with fearless honesty, the temptation to get caught up with
ideas of simplicity, poverty and silence rather than living
the experience itself. In this his experience has echoes
of the Western desert spirituality that so inspired him as
a young man and which, as we saw at the beginning of
this book, cradled the first ideas of confession in Christian
consciousness.

Like Wittgenstein, he saw by now that his old enemy – the
theologizing of what were in themselves radical experiences beyond language – had to be resisted. This solitude
would ultimately take him beyond all religious structures,
whether Hindu or Christian, to the place he variously
called 'the source', 'I AM' or 'the ground'. All that was left
for him was what he called the 'osmosis of prayer' where
'the ultimate correspondences – *Upanishads* – are revealed
between the mystery of Christ and that of the Purusha'.[66]
Ultimately his goal was a 'stripping' – mentally, physically
and spiritually – until nothing was left except the raw
encounter with the source; this was the true solitude, the

true poverty: 'Be ready to live in my cave to the end of my life, with no one taking any special care for me or showering me with marks of esteem and honour, obliged to beg each midday for my handful of rice.'[67]

Such a total poverty – mental, spiritual and physical – was best expressed for Swamiji by the Indian ideal of the *sannyāsi*. From as early as 1952, shortly after his encounter with Arunāchala, Swami Abhishiktananda was fascinated by the Hindu concept of *sannyāsa*. As he wrote in his diary in that year:

> The *sannyāsī* has no friends in the proper sense of the word. He has effectively renounced all affections, familial and other ... that is why the *shastras* forbid the *sannyāsī* to stay more than a few days in the same place. His heart should not be caught by any snare ...
>
> I will not be a genuine *sannyāsī* until the day when I am able, without the least distress or fear, to see the loss, in a strange if not downright hostile environment, of all help, all affection, all respect. And that too, on the supposition that I could no longer return to my other life (with its friendships, the priesthood and financial and moral support).[68]

This striking, if not grim, description of *sannyāsa* pits its demands against every certainty and comfort the young priest had ever known, and it was an ideal he would pursue for the rest of his life in India. From an early stage Abhishiktananda asked the question: 'Does Hindu *sannyāsa* really have an equivalent in Christianity?',[69] and much of the rest of his life would be dedicated to exploring this goal. As we have seen, after Arunāchala he became increasingly preoccupied with the silence, solitude and poverty which he felt lay at the heart of *sannyāsa*, which for him became a complete stripping, a complete emptying: '*Sannyāsa* involves not only withdrawal from society, from the social and religious framework, from social and religious obligations etc., but also a fundamental commitment beyond the intellectual framework of one's life.'[70]

We could argue that Abhishiktananda's '*sannyāsa*' was even more extreme than the Hindu version. The Hindu tradition involves a ritualized stripping away prescribed for certain castes (and indeed genders) only.[71] What Abhishiktananda was advocating, even at this early stage, was something far more radical – it was a '*sannyāsa* beyond *sannyāsa*' – a stripping away that also included the stripping away of all (what he saw as) unnecessary religious accoutrements.[72] In 1954 he wrote in his diary that it was the renouncing of 'the *nāmarūpa* of himself and of God ... *sannyāsa*, in its total renunciation and its total liberation, is incompatible with ecclesial Christianity, which does not admit the possibility of itself being transcended'.[73] In 1954 it was the transcendence of Christianity that preoccupied him. Twenty years later in his last written essay, on *sannyāsa*, he describes it as the 'renunciation of renunciation' – it would for him ultimately go beyond every religious form, including Hinduism. At this last stage of his life, it is 'beyond all dharma, including all ethical and religious duties'.[74] His renunciation was that of the 'old ones', 'the hairy ones' (*keśi*) described in the *Ṛg Veda* who predate the niceties of the *Upanishads* and their fine-tuned Brahmanic teaching. No doubt this attitude was inspired

by the wild (and possibly psychotic) *rishis* he met on the
banks of the Ganges in his own final period of renunciation. At this stage there is no theology or learning left;
such a person has become what he calls a 'fire *sannyāsi*'[75]
who 'becomes indifferent, on that very day he should go
forth and roam'.[76]

Yet Abhishiktananda could never leave his French intellectual discrimination entirely behind (both in the text of
Sannyasa and in his letters he explains how the other swamis
looked at the number of books in his cell with amazement
– such books, they announced, should not be necessary for
a true renouncer). In April 1973, in his last year, he wrote
to his new disciple, Marc Chaduc: 'But is not our "idea" of
sannyasa terribly idealistic, perhaps beyond what is really
possible? But even so, there is a place for such acosmics in the
cosmos, on the margin … at the edge of a village or a forest.'[77]

Just as Wittgenstein's self-examination through his
confession had led him to the edge of philosophy and
logical reasoning, so too Abhishiktananda's confessional
quest led to a silence beyond all forms. Even, dare we say
it, a spirituality beyond all spiritualities.

THE FINAL YEARS: DEVOTION, KNOWLEDGE
AND ACTION

As it turned out, Abhishiktananda had difficulty living
in isolation at Gyansu, spending half the year there and
the other half teaching and travelling in the Indian plains.
After his heart attack in July 1973 he realized he would
never live in his 'cave' again and died later that year in a
nursing home at Indore. His disciple Marc Chaduc, a

young French seminarian for whom much of the last essay *Sannyasa* was written (and which he edited), attempted to live the ideal of the '*sannyāsa* beyond *sannyāsa*', only to vanish in 1977 and never be heard of again.[78] As one of his admirers, the Anglican missionary Murray Rogers, later told Abhishiktananda's biographer Shirley du Boulay in an interview in 2004:

> If these experiences were too strong for Swamiji, with his long years of monastic life, with so many years of maturation, physically and spiritually, would it be surprising for Ajatananda (Marc Chaduc's adopted name), in his thirties and with no years of monastic training and experience, to have been overwhelmed by what had happened to him in the deepest depth of his being? Had Swamiji, for whom this area of spiritual fatherhood was also an unknown mystery, for whom his hopes had been more wonderfully fulfilled than he could have dared to hope and pray, failed to give sufficient weight to the danger, human and spiritual, laid on Ajatananda?[79]

Whatever happened to his disciple, Abhishiktananda himself was clearly conflicted in his notion of how to live his 'Christian-*advaita*' experience, especially as to the form it should take.

Abhishiktananda's way thus ultimately became a 'path beyond all paths'. In his lonely journey he set out to transcend all religious forms. Yet this path seemed to some others harsh and inhuman. We have already mentioned the criticism of his ability to foster his disciple Marc. The Swiss ambassador to India, Jacques-Albert Cuttat, had met the

Swami in the early 1960s and asked him to initiate a series of conversations between Hindus and Christians sponsored by his office (the discussions would later be published as 'Hindu-Christian Meeting Point'). Yet this promising dialogue would end abruptly in 1963. Commenting on Abhishiktananda and his way, Dr Cuttat later wrote:

> Suddenly I realised that something essential was lacking in this *jnanic* way to the Supreme.[80] Everything whatsoever was pervaded with joy and bliss centred in my own Self, the whole reality was luminous and transparent, yet all this happiness was without *love*. There is in this way neither love for God nor love to the other, both are not loved as *others*. Swami Abhishiktananda lives in a happy world of *sacred solitude* ... I became incapable to follow again the way of Swami Abhishiktananda.[81]

Abhishiktananda's way was certainly not a way that the majority of Christians (or Hindus) could comfortably follow. Yet, as he moved more into isolation at the end of his life, this seemed to him irrelevant. As he wrote in 1956: 'whoever has once had the "taste" of *advaita* on his tongue, no longer enjoys the flavour of anything else'.[82] He was impelled from his first encounter with a fire, the fire of the beyond, that would ultimately consume him.[83]

THE FIRE OF CHRIST

As this chapter has demonstrated, to judge Abhishiktananda by the standards of accepted religions is ultimately a fool's errand. After Arunāchala his preoccupation with such conventional 'religious' expectations – even regarding the Christian ashram Shantivanam he had founded with Fr Monchanin – simply dropped away. Ultimately he was left with a 'scorching fire' that burnt away all religious forms, ideas and duties. This fire, recorded in some of his last confessional diary entries and letters, constellated for him around the nature of our relationship with Christ – not *bhakti* devotion or *karmic* action, or even indeed the *jnanic* 'knowledge of God', but the channel by which we are scorched by the fire of encounter with the Beyond. Increasingly he would characterize this encounter as a 'nuclear explosion' that blows apart all certainties: 'Christianity is neither knowledge, nor devotion, nor ethics and ritual – nor is it duty, religion – (formulas, institutions). It is an explosion of the Spirit. It accepts any religious basis (*jñana*, *bhakti/karma*) to the extent necessary in each case.'[84]

As he entered into this encounter at the end of his life, words and writing began to fail him. Even as he checked proofs of *Sagesse* he complained that he no longer accepted its thesis of a Christian theology of 'fulfillment' of *advaita*. He went on, in a letter to his disciple Marc, to question: 'But how to tell, pass on, this truth? For this truth is not conceptual. The value of words that I was able to speak to you last year lay in their *resonance* rather than in their immediate meaning. Once conceptualized, this truth which I bear is no longer true.'[85]

As he approached the encounter he had long sought, he increasingly moved into poetry, as he had done from his early Arunāchala days (and in conscious imitation of his great inspiration, St John of the Cross), for once again we

are at Wittgenstein's point of 'saying and showing' where
words dissolve in the spindrift of the Beyond:

> In the depth of the heart,
> In the deepest darkness
> A solitary flame has blazed up.
> Who will tell the secret of the flame
> The mystery of the One
> The mystery of the Three?
> He alone will know it
> Who will never again be able to tell it
> Having fallen into the flame
> And in it been consumed.[86]

In his last letters he identified the experience with that of
Christ's relation to the Father, 'scorched' by the encounter:

> It seems in his Baptism he (Christ) had an overwhelming
> experience; he felt himself to be Son, not in a notional,
> Greek fashion, but that he had a commission given by
> Yahweh to fulfil; and in this commission he felt his near-
> ness to Yahweh ... It is the reduction of the mystery
> of Jesus to a Jewish or Greek concept that makes the
> dialogue of salvation with non-Christians so difficult.
> One culture has monopolised Jesus. He has been turned
> into an idea. People argue about Jesus – it is easier to let
> yourself be scorched by contact with him.[87]

Ironically, Abhishiktananda was destined to receive his own
'scorching' shortly after writing this letter. In July 1973,
having initiated his disciple Marc into sannyāsa on the banks

of the Ganges, he spent some days of ecstatic communion with him in a deserted Shaivite temple. On 12 July he went into Rishikesh to buy provisions for the two, when he suffered a near-fatal heart attack as he ran for a bus. He was fortunately spotted by another French lady some time later and was able to be nursed in Indore for the next few months before dying in December 1973. Shortly after the experience, which he later described as being beyond life and death, he wrote a poem to his beloved disciple:

> MARC,
> Shiva's column of fire
> brushed against me
> Saturday midday
> In the bazaar at Rishikesh,
> and I still do not understand
> why it did not carry me off.
> Joy, the serene one,
> OM *tat sat* (*That – Brahman – is the Real*)
> *Ekadrishi* (the one-pointed gaze)
> *Ekarshi* (the unique rishi)
> Oh!
> The crowning grace
> OM!
> With my love.[88]

In the time remaining he often returned to his Breton origins and the Celtic myths we explored in Chapter Two by referring to the encounter as the 'discovery of the Grail'. As he wrote to his sister shortly after his collapse: 'I have found the GRAIL! And this extra lease of life – for such it is – can only be used for living and sharing this discovery.'[89]

Encountering the mythic qualities that lie close to the sources of the soul, he had recourse, as we did in earlier chapters, to the discourse of the Celtic Arthurian legend to give shape to his final discourse:

> The Grail is a marvellous symbol, that old myth around which have coalesced a heap of pagan Celtic and later, Christian myths. With many others Galahad caught the fragrance of the Grail, with Bors and Perceval he drank of it, and one day it was given to him alone to openly see within it … The Grail is neither far nor near, it is free from all location.[90]

It is poignant that as he lay dying in the Indore hospital, having received his long-awaited realization on the banks of the Ganges, he returned to his Celtic-Breton roots. Like the wounded Lord Tristan dying on the shores of his native Brittany, Swamiji found the perfect symbol for that which he freely now saw went beyond the concepts and theologies not only of Christianity but also of Hinduism. As he confided in one of his last diary entries:

> I have found the Grail. And that is what I keep saying and writing to anyone who can grasp the figure of speech. The quest for the Grail is basically nothing else than the quest for the Self. A single quest that is the meaning of all the myths and symbols. It is yourself that you are seeking through everything. And in this quest you run about everywhere whereas the Grail is here, close at hand, you only have to open your eyes.[91]

Swamiji's transcendent Tristan wound seemed to have finally been healed in the symbolic language of the *mythos*. Three months later, on 7 December 1973, he underwent what he termed 'the great departure' – *mahāprasthāna* – to the abode of great silence.[92]

ABHISHIKTANANDA'S SMILE

We began our chapter with the description of the joyful encounter with Swamiji by one of his students – 'a jester in the Court of God'. For, despite the severity of his discipline and the austerity of the path he underwent, all who knew him commented on Swamiji's ability to smile at himself no matter what vicissitudes he encountered (the dry Gallic humour of an unrepentant son of Descartes no doubt helped him here). He was often touched by the Indian notion of *līlā* – the divine play of God in creation.[93] Like a prophet, Swamiji anticipated the challenges of our twenty-first-century encounters between the world's great faiths. For him this must not be a cause of despair but an occasion to 'smile':

> Our time is one of those without precedent in the history of the world, when the worldwide coming together makes us clearly see that we ourselves and our whole tradition and every tradition are essentially conditioned ...
>
> We find ourselves once more Christian, Hindu, Buddhist, for each one has his own line of development, marked out already from his mother's lap. But we also have to 'smile'. Not a smile which looks down condescendingly from above, still less a smile of mockery, but one which is simply an opening out, like the flower unfolding its petals.[94]

From this perspective of the divine *līlā*, all the efforts of religion to 'pin down' the divine, not least those of his own Catholic Church, made him smile. As he wrote in 1963 during the meeting of the Second Vatican Council to reform the Catholic Church:

> So the Council meets again and they are going to be serious. And bishops in cope and mitre are going to decide about God. And the observers in suits are going to check their decisions. What a laugh!
>
> There must surely be an angel called 'The Laugh of God'. It is he who is the greatest amongst them, the Great Laugh of God, when he looks down on human beings, human beings who with all the seriousness of a 'butler' lay the table for God and get ready to serve him.[95]

Abhishiktananda's confessions – expressed in such exquisite detail in his private diaries and letters – reveal the spirit of his Breton maritime ancestors. A bold traveller, from the moment he set foot in India he was determined, like Walt Whitman, to 'reach the further shore', for he was 'bound where mariner has not yet dared to go' and dared 'risk the ship, ourselves and all'. Ultimately, with Whitman, he could declare, 'O daring joy, but safe! are they not all the seas of God?' Swamiji's last enigmatic smile was the smile of one who had finally found the land he had been searching for.

CHAPTER FIVE

CONFESSIONS OF FIRE:
ST JOHN OF THE CROSS

Flame, alive, compelling,
yet tender past all telling,
reaching the secret center of my soul!
Since now evasion's over,
finish your work, my Lover,
break the last thread,
wound me and make me whole!
Burn that is for my healing!
Wound of delight past feeling!
Ah, gentle hand whose touch is a caress,
foretaste of heaven conveying
and every debt repaying:
slaying, you give me life for death's distress.
O lamps of fire bright-burning
with splendid brilliance, turning
deep caverns of my soul to pools of light!
Once shadowed, dim, unknowing,
now their strange new-found glowing
gives warmth and radiance for my Love's delight.
Ah, gentle and so loving
you wake within me, proving
that you are there in secret, all alone;

your fragrant breathing stills me
your grace, your glory fills me
so tenderly your love becomes my own.[1]

A TRACE OF THE DIVINE

I have felt somewhat reluctant, most noble and devout lady, to explain these four stanzas, as you asked, since they deal with such interior and spiritual matters, for which communication language normally fails (as spirit transcends sense) and I consequently find it difficult to say anything of substance on the matter. Also, it is difficult to speak well of the intimate depths of the spirit (*entrañas del espíritu*, literally 'entrails of the spirit') if one doesn't inhabit those depths oneself. And as I have not done that much up to now I have delayed writing about these matters. But now the Lord has appeared to grant me a little knowledge and given me a little fire ... I feel encouraged knowing for certain that by my own power I can say little of value, especially regarding such sublime and important matters.[2]

So begins the commentary by St John of the Cross on his last, and possibly greatest, poem, *The Living Flame of Love*. The poem was probably written sometime between May 1585 and April 1587 (according to the testimony of Juan Evangelista, he only took a fortnight to write it) while he was Prior of the Convent of Los Martires in Granada under the shadow of the magnificent Sierra Nevada and Alhambra

Palace.³ The preamble to his explanation above resembles the prologue to the last work of his equally famous co-worker and spiritual associate, St Teresa of Avila. John had arrived in Granada in 1582, the year of Teresa's death, and I don't think it is too fanciful to suggest that in this, his last great poem, he recalls the indomitable spirit of the great Teresa, whose shade often hovers over the pages. For had she now not reached the place of bliss of which they had both spoken during their long and eventful collaboration together? She began her last masterpiece, *The Interior Castle*, thus:

> Few things which I have been ordered to undertake under obedience have been as difficult as this present task: to write about the matter of prayer. Because, for one reason, the Lord doesn't seem to be giving me the spirit or desire to do it. For another, for three months now I have had noises and weakness in the head that have been so great that I find it hard even to write about pressing business matters. However I know that the strength that arises from obedience has a way of simplifying matters that seem impossible, the will is determined to attempt this task even though the prospect makes my nature suffer a lot; for the Lord hasn't given me enough virtue to enable me to continually wrestle both with sickness and occupations of many kinds without feeling a great aversion to such a task.⁴

Both saints approached their last and possibly greatest tasks with equal aversion. Teresa complained of 'noises in her head' which meant she couldn't even attend to the necessary business of running a newly created religious order, while John was fearful of his own spiritual immaturity as he attempted to write of such matters. Both protestations are belied, of course, by the masterpieces that they then went on to produce. Yet I feel it might be a mistake to pass over these first protests too quickly. If such renowned spiritual masters challenge the whole task of writing about spirituality, shouldn't we pay attention to this? As much as Wittgenstein, Abhishiktananda, Freud or Augustine did, they stand on the abyss of unknowing that opens up with alarming rapidity when we stare into our souls, seeking to map that abyss with the tentative stutterings of language. The 'I-know-not-what behind the stammering' of John's *Spiritual Canticle*.[5] For, as I indicated earlier, as we regard the unknown depths of the soul we must often resort to the companions of unknowing – the poetic, the imaginative and the mythic – to give voice to what we find there. This will be John's path.

In these last three chapters we have canvassed three responses to the Tristan wound of the modern soul. We saw in Chapter Three how Ludwig Wittgenstein opened the door to the transcendent but would not step through it. In Chapter Four we followed Henri Le Saux's journey from reluctant missionary to one 'who had found the Grail' as he fell into the abyss. In this final chapter we find ourselves in the Grail Castle itself as we listen to the incomparable poetry of St John of the Cross. At this point of entry to the transcendent he declares: 'There is a certain "I don't know what" which is felt yet remains to be said, a thing which is known but remains to be described, a trace of the divine discovered by the soul which God has left to track Him down …'[6] It is as if having entered the Grail Castle only poetry will now suffice to convey what is happening.

Using the language and imagery of the hunt, John speaks of a divine trace or scent (*un subido rastro que se descubre al alma de Dios quedándose por rastrear*) which we have caught on the early-morning air – *this* alone (the 'I don't know what') will lead us to the Divine. It is, as he continues, 'a love that wounds the soul', an outstanding experience that really cannot be put into words. It is Abhishiktananda's 'Grail' experienced outside the bus station of Rishikesh; it is Wittgenstein's fire of longing felt in the lonely dark nights of Norway: 'One of the outstanding favours God grants briefly in this life is an understanding and experience of Himself so lucid and lofty as to make one know clearly that He cannot be completely understood or experienced.'[7]

John's *Living Flame* is thus his final confession and testament as he goes 'gently into that good night'. A testimonial made not to a priest or bishop, or even to a discalced friar, but to a simple 'unlettered' laywoman – Doña Ana del Mercado y Peñalosa. Born in Segovia, to which she would return with John to found his convent there, she was at this time widowed and living in Granada with her brother. John's final testament is made to a woman, and it is to a woman's heart that he confides his last attempts at spiritual writing.

Throughout the work, John struggles with the boundary of what can be said and what can be shown every bit as much as the other confessors we have explored in this book. His struggle will end, one hundred pages later, with reiterations of the position he began with – that the nature of self lies on the mysterious boundary of what can be said and what cannot be uttered: 'Of this breath of God I would not wish to speak, nor will I: for I see clearly that I do not know how to and it would appear less than it is if I spoke about it.'[8]

What, then, is this mystery at the heart of the human person with which John struggles throughout his confession? John indicates what this is in the first verse of the poem:

Flame, alive, compelling,
yet tender past all telling,
reaching the secret centre of my soul![9]

The 'living flame', the ecstasy to which the poem directs our gaze, occurs, says John, in the 'substance of our soul' (*en la substancia del alma*) – the place where, to use his delightful phrase, the 'fiesta of the Holy Spirit' takes place (*esta fiesta del Espíritu Santo*), making the centre of the soul seem more like a Spanish plaza ready for a party! It is a 'place' that is marked by '*deleite*/delight' as much as by any theological virtue[10]: 'the delight (*deleite*) and pleasure (*gozar*) of the soul and spirit are so much greater because God does all the work without the soul having to do anything'.[11] The self at this moment is at a passive point where its whole *raison d'être* is to receive gifts and joys from the Spirit 'in the depths' (*en el fondo del alma*). We are once again at the place of divine play – *līlā* – so beloved of Abhishiktananda.

The soul, *el alma*, is, for John, not a hard physical metaphor or spatial entity. Using his precise scholastic language, he disabuses us of this illusion:

Being a spirit, the soul neither has height or depth, nor deeper or less deep within it as do quantitative bodies. As it has no parts, it doesn't have differences between the inner and outer, for all is of one manner and *it doesn't have a centre of depth and less depth quantitatively speaking*.[12]

John is making the simple and essential point that quantitative language will dissolve when we talk about mind and soul. The great error, for him, is, when speaking of mental or spiritual entities, we try to use spatial (or what he calls 'quantitative') metaphors. The 'centre of the soul' thus becomes for him a provisional word for all that can be reached by the natural capacities and power of the person involved.[13] This is the place of the 'fiestas of the Holy Spirit' – the plaza at the centre of the soul where the divine *līlā* will sport itself.

As we approach the centre, says John, we encounter the same moment described by St Augustine in Chapter One earlier: that is we discover there the divine Trinity that we have been seeking outside for so long. This dissolution of the individual centre into the embrace of the Divine means that at the heart of ourselves lies mystery – God will always be greater than anything we claim God to be. *Ipso facto* – I, my soul, will always be greater than anything I can grasp, for *el centro del alma*, 'the centre of the soul', is God, '*es Dios*'.[14] At this point we shall 'know, love and enjoy' God in his divine *līlā*.[15] This will be the point at which 'the Most Blessed Trinity will come and dwell' within the soul by 'divinely illuminating its intellect with the wisdom of the Son, delighting its will in the Holy Spirit and by absorbing it powerfully and mightily in the abyss of the Father's sweet embrace' (*y absorbiéndola el Padre ponderosa y fuertemente en el abrazo abisal de su dulzura*).[16] This union with God can only happen, says John, outside of this life, for on earth we do not have the capacity to reach that point.

The journey of the soul to God, in this life at least, is for John a never-ending one. One that is marked with dynamism and movement where the soul should not feel 'satisfied'.[17] Constantly, he tells us, the soul 'goes out unseen',[18] 'in darkness and security', and searches for the beloved who has 'hidden and left me moaning'.[19] John's view of the human person is of an arena (for the fiestas?) of constant searching and striving. We are never at rest on this earth as we seek the 'fast God, always before us and leaving as we arrive'.[20] As with Teresa, John advocates Christian life as a continual process of de-centring rather than centring. In fact, we could conclude from his account that the more secure we are in our 'centre' the further we are from our Beloved: 'although it is in its centre, it is not yet in its deepest, for it can go deeper in God'.[21]

Like Teresa, John presents a generous God who is always calling us to this delightful place and delightful road, and John reinforces his point by quoting Proverbs 8.31 (as Teresa does at the beginning of her *Interior Castle*) where he states that God 'does not hesitate to find his delights (*deleites*) with the children of men in common throughout the whole earth'.[22] For 'the father of Light', he asserts, is not 'tight-fisted' with his favours but is always dispensing them abundantly without 'being a respecter of persons'.[23] Our whole journey to God, then (which for John is also our journey to ourselves), is a journey through 'degrees of love'[24] where the more deeply we unite with God the more deeply we experience love.

For John, however, this love is also a 'love-wound' – a 'happy wound'[25] (reflecting the Catholic Easter *Exsultet* hymn: *O Felix Culpa!* – 'O Happy Fault!') – 'wrought by one who knows only how to heal it', 'made only for delight (*regalo*)'. Getting more ecstatic as he writes, John suggests that the wound is infinite and made for infinite delight as the infinite fire of love burns out 'the infinite centre of the soul' (*el infinito centro*), 'burning all that is combustible so that all that can be caressed is delighted!' (*abrasando todo lo que se pudo abrasar, para regalar todo lo que se pudo regalar*). We have returned to the sickbed of Lord Tristan that we left in Chapter Two, but now the terrible wound has been transfigured. Finally it has been touched 'at the infinite centre of the soul' with the transcendent touch of the Divine so that the ecstatic libidinal joy and love can flow once again. There is no 'love potion' for John as he tastes now the real thing.

THE LIBIDINAL SOURCES OF CONFESSION

As we have seen throughout this book, the sources of confession will often lie close to the libidinal sources of the self. The confessional act requires honesty and openness to the secret libidinal sources of the self – what John calls 'the interior wine-cellar' (*la interior bodega*) in the *Spiritual Canticle*.[26] Reminding us here that 'one can say nothing about it just as one can say nothing about God himself that resembles Him',[27] we are faced with the libidinal mystery that lies at the centre of our human being. The same libidinal centre that fascinated all our seekers – from Augustine to Freud alike.

Faced with this libidinal centre of the human person in ecstatic love poetry such as John's, we find two approaches among the commentators (and this is nothing new; the same interpretations continue to recur throughout the five hundred years of commentary on the writings of John and his co-worker Teresa of Avila).[28] The first, so well demonstrated in many pious commentaries, is to downplay or misplace the clear libidinal element in his writing. That it is there cannot be denied. What mystifies many commentators is *why* it should be there in the first place. This is simply answered. John is heir to the medieval tradition of Dionysian *theologia mystica* which, taking its cue from Plato, emphasized the role of *eros* in enacting the erotic union with the divine that is vouchsafed to all seekers of the divine. As this tradition is so rarely studied today (John, importantly, received an award for his essay on Dionysius as a student at Salamanca University), we no longer have the tools to appreciate the erotico-mystical milieu within which John and Teresa (and most of their contemporaries) were working.[29]

Allied to this tendency to bleach the work of John of all its erotico-mystical content is the other tendency, which we can call broadly the reductionist one. Taking its cue from Freud, alas, it seeks to portray the mystical writing of John and Teresa as purely erotic without any recognition of the Platonic milieu from which it arises. The chief artefact of this school is Bernini's 'Teresa in Ecstasy' at Santa Maria della Vittoria in Rome. This famous statue, which has launched so many jejune theses on Teresa that treat her as 'hysteric', is the opposite reaction to what has just been described. Such interpretations see the erotic language within both Teresa and John but are unable, sadly, to appreciate its origins within the late-medieval tradition of *theologia mystica*. Psychology, proud of its independence, rarely stoops to sully itself in the dubious world of the spirit from which, ultimately, it derives.

This spiritual–biological divide we can class, sadly, as yet another manifestation of the Tristan wound, as Western culture has sought to divide the one from the other. The genius of a writer such as John, and the reason I have devoted this final chapter to him, is that he is able to bridge that gap. Thus, returning to his 'caressing wound', John pronounces:

> There is another and most sublime way of cauterizing the soul and it comes about in this manner: it will come about that when the soul is inflamed in this love, although not as inflamed as the love just mentioned, (yet it is fitting that it be so for what I want to say) – it will feel that a seraph is assailing it by means of an arrow or dart that is totally inflamed with love. And the seraph pierces and cauterizes this soul that like a red-hot coal, or better a flame, is already enkindled. And then in this cauterization, when the soul is transpierced with that dart, the flame gushes forth fiercely and with a sudden ascent, like the fire in a furnace or an oven when someone uses a poker or bellows to stir and excite it. And being wounded by this fiery dart, the soul feels the wound with unsurpassable delight. Besides being fully stirred in great sweetness by the blowing or impetuous motion of the seraph, in which it feels in its intense ardor to be dissolving in love, it is aware of the delicate wound and the herb (which serves as a keen temper to the dart) as though it were a sharp point in the substance of the spirit, in the heart of the pierced soul.[30]

Here once again we are reminded of the ecstatic libidinal scene in Chapter 29 of Teresa's *Life* where Teresa encountered the cherub with the wounding spear (consequently used as the inspiration for Bernini's statue):

> Sometimes (when I was at this place) the Lord wanted me to see this vision: I saw an angel close to me on

my left side in corporeal form, something I only see occasionally. Although angels are represented to me many times I don't see them, at least not in the sense of 'vision' of which I spoke at first. It pleased the Lord that I should see this vision in the following manner: he was not large but small, very beautiful, the face so enflamed that he appeared to be one of the very high angels that appear to be totally aflame (I believe they are called Cherubim although they don't tell me their names, but I see clearly that there is a great difference between certain types of angels and others, and between these and others still, of a kind that I could not possibly explain). I saw in his hands a long golden spear (*un dardo de oro largo*), and at the end of the iron tip there appeared a little flame, this he seemed to put into my heart several times so that it reached my entrails (*y que me llegava a las entrañas*).[31] As he removed it, they seemed to be drawn with it so that I was left totally on fire with a great love of God. The pain I felt was so great that I uttered several moans, and so excessive was the sweetness (*suavidad*) caused by this pain that one would never want to lose it, nor would the soul be content with anything less than God. It is not a bodily pain, but spiritual, although the body has a share in it – considerably so. It is such a sweet love-exchange (*un requiebro*) which passes between the soul and God that I beg Him out of His goodness to give this *gusto* to anyone who thinks I am lying.[32]

John began his commentary on the *Flame* by saying that he had insufficient experience of the 'spiritual entrails' to write the book. Was he thinking here of this famous description from Teresa's *Life* repeated before her death in the Sixth Mansions of her *Interior Castle*?[33] In my earlier *Teresa of Avila: Doctor of the Soul* I argued how in both passages Teresa demonstrates her debt to the mystical theology tradition to which she is heir by her precise use of the language and terminology of that tradition. The flame of the cherubim (John, possibly more theologically correct, replaces it with the 'flame of the Seraphim') belongs firmly in the Victorine tradition that did so much to shape the *theologia mystica* as evidenced, for example, in the 'dart of flaming love' in the anonymous English *Cloud of Unknowing* and clearly referenced in John's account. In the *Interior Castle* Teresa introduces the all-important word *centella* – a clear reference to the *synderesis* of the medieval mystical tradition (literally; 'the little spark'): the place, according to Jean Gerson, St Bonaventure and Hugh of Balma (and ultimately derived from Augustine), where the divine touches the human in the soul. This little spark gently 'touches' the heart and causes the ecstasy of fire. Teresa's 'little spark' becomes a raging inferno in John's parallel account where we read of a 'little coal' enkindling the oven from which a flame 'gushes forth, vehemently and with sudden ascent'. As with Teresa, the fiery dart wounds and delights in equal measure, as it should. For unlike a dodgy post-Freudian reductionism or a bland pious bleaching, the true account of John's and Teresa's ecstasy is the necessary juxtaposition of the libidinal and the spiritual at the centre of the human personality. This is the heart of desire and it returns us once again to where we began this book – with the Tristan wound at the heart of the modern soul and the need for psycho-spiritual healing.

In a way this shouldn't surprise us. For as well as the birth of confession and the writing of the Celtic-Christian myths at the start of the thirteenth century that we described earlier, the same period saw not only the birth of the *theologia mystica* that John and Teresa used to articulate their sense of the erotico-mystical nature of human personhood but also the birth of the religious order to which they both belonged – the Carmelites. For John and Teresa's Carmel also began in that fateful decade at the beginning of the thirteenth century just as Gottfried was writing his *Tristan* in Strasbourg and the Council Fathers were delineating the nature of confession in Rome. At this point the founding fathers of the order of Carmel came together to establish the order on Mount Carmel near present-day Haifa in Israel.

THE STORY OF CARMEL

The Carmelite order traces its origins to the Jewish 'School of the Prophets' traditionally established by Elijah on the sides of Mount Carmel. Varied etymologies are suggested for the origins of the word, including that it derives from the words *krm* and *l,* suggesting 'a vineyard'; others include 'a scrubby area'. Today it remains a green verdant place that dominates the Mediterranean landscape for miles around. As well as its Jewish and Christian associations, for the Muslims it is associated with *Khidr* – 'The Green One' or 'Verdant One', another name given to Elijah in this tradition. Thus the cave of Elijah, situated adjacent to the present-day Carmelite Priory of 'Stella Maris', and currently a synagogue, has during its 2,500-year existence been a church, a mosque, a synagogue and possibly a Roman shrine.[34]

Carmel is frequently mentioned in the Jewish Scriptures, perhaps most famously in the Song of Songs 7.5: 'Your head crowns you like Carmel and your flowing locks are like purple.' It is the place where Elijah performs some of the most important acts of his ministry, in particular the fight with the prophets of Baal[35] and the prophecy from the cloud in the sea. His final taking up in the fiery chariot watched by Elisha[36] is said to have inspired the original habits of the Carmelite order, which were streaked to represent the cinders from the chariot scorching their robes.

Historically the origins of the order are cloudy. The eleventh and twelfth centuries had seen the first significant medieval encounter between Islam and Christianity, known as 'The Crusades', begin with the First Crusade preached by Pope Urban II in 1095 at Clermont-Ferrand in France, and continuing throughout the twelfth century. By the early thirteenth century, as the rules of confession were being formulated in Europe and Gottfried wrote his *Tristan*, we begin to hear the first reports of groups of former Crusaders settling on the 'Holy Mountain' near the Wadi 'ain es-Siah associated with Elijah. Thus we find Jacques de Vitry, Bishop of nearby Acre, writing around 1216:

> Others after the example and in imitation of the holy solitary Elijah, the Prophet, lived as hermits in the beehives of small cells on Mount Carmel ... near the spring which is called the Spring of Elijah ... Where in little comb-like cells these bees of the Lord laid up sweet spiritual honey.[37]

It was this disparate group, of whom we know so little, who approached Albert of Vercelli, Patriarch of Jerusalem, for a Rule sometime between 1206 and 1214. This Rule, the original form of which is not known,[38] was finally promulgated by Pope Innocent IV in his 1247 Bull *Quae honorem conditoris*.[39] After 1214 the fortunes of the young order underwent another twist as increasing Muslim incursions into the Christian lands around Acre had made it necessary for the group of hermits to leave the Holy Land in 1238. Arriving in Europe, new communities of the Order were first established at Cyprus, Messina (Sicily) and Aylesford and Hulne in England, home of the original Tristan legend. John was therefore heir to an order also created during those eventful early decades of the thirteenth century. Yet, in opposition to the growing secular/spiritual divide presaged by the thirteenth century, we see in the writings of John what we might call a 'third way' between the overly secular and the purely transcendent, and nowhere is this clearer than in John's ecstatic confessions of fire.

THE HEALING OF THE WOUND

Earlier in this book we described the 'Tristan wound' inflicted upon the Western soul at the beginning of the modern period. As I described the ailing Tristan lying on his bed – wounded, paralysed and unable to move – I argued that his wound was the 'transcendent wound' of the modern Western soul. In the past three chapters we have explored three confessions and how they may offer a way forward to the healing of the Western *psyche*. With Wittgenstein we saw the possibility, through confession, of opening a door to the transcendent. In the diaries of Abhishiktananda we encountered a 'spirituality beyond spiritualities' as he embraced the abyss of the heart. Finally, with our last confessor, St John of the Cross, we see the abyss of the heart opening up into the flame of the transcendent – the 'living flame of love' conveyed in his incomparable poetic-confessions. Accordingly, I would like to end our journey following the wanderings of the modern soul in its search for healing by arguing that John, in his spiritual anthropology and poetry, offers us a way through the pain of desire and confession for the healing of the transcendent wound within us all. This he delineates with the skill and precision of a surgeon applying his heal- ing arts to the wounded patient and it is to his confessional art that we turn in conclusion.

JOHN'S HEALING OF THE SOUL

As a student, John was educated at the newly established Jesuit college of Medina del Campo and so would have been familiar with the ethos and training of St Ignatius of Loyola's *Spiritual Exercises*. Like John, Ignatius lived at the birth of our modern age in that transition period of the sixteenth-century Golden Age in Spanish history where the two worlds of the medieval and the modern collided. Brought up with a great love of the practice of military arts, the young Iñigo (as Ignatius was called at this time) had an opportunity to display his skills in this arena when a large French army besieged the town of Pamplona in 1521.[40] Despite unwillingness among his confrères, the young Iñigo urged a futile resistance to the French, revealing the stubborn pride that lay deep in his character. In the battle of 17 May a cannonball shattered one of his legs as it passed between them. He retired wounded from the battle and was taken back to the family castle, arriving in June 1521, aged thirty.

In late middle age, like so many of the contributors to this book, Ignatius, as he was now called, was persuaded, somewhat reluctantly, to embark upon a series of confessional 'Reminiscences'. No Augustine or Freud, the middle-aged Ignatius was never entirely comfortable in either Latin or indeed Spanish. Brodrick suggests that as Iñigo's first language was Basque, he had difficulty speaking in his adopted Castilian and famously found the learning of Latin excruciating.[41] Roland Barthes goes further to describe Ignatius, along with the Marquis de Sade, as a 'logothete' who creates a new architecture of language.[42] Thus, as he dictated his 'Reminiscences' to Luis Goncalves da Câmara in Rome in the 1550s, we hear the by now familiar confessional voice of a man struggling to articulate his innermost desires to another listener.

Recalling his youthful antics in this account, Ignatius tells us that in the boredom of convalescence he asked for romantic books of chivalry to while away the time as he lay in the family castle of Loyola. Instead, the only books available were a *Life of Christ / Vita Christi* by the Carthusian Ludolf of Saxony, and a collection of lives of the saints: *The Golden Legend* by the Dominican Jacobus de Voragine (d. 1298), translated into Castillian in a 1511 Toledan edition called *Flos Sanctorum / The Flowers of the Saints*. In his preface to this book, the Cistercian Gauberto Vagad wrote that the saints were 'the knights of God' who did resplendent deeds 'in the service of the eternal Prince, Christ Jesus' under whose 'victorious banner' they assembled.

We can see already how these military metaphors would have appealed to the young hot-head Iñigo, and the idea of embarking upon military service to Christ under the banner of the King would stay with him for the rest of his life. From now on he resolved that rather than following the chivalrous service of high-born ladies he would dedicate his energies to becoming a 'knight of Christ'.

If this were all, then Iñigo would probably have become another footnote of the great outpouring of early-sixteenth-century Spanish piety. Yet this young man was more complicated, and ultimately more interesting, than a prancing dandy who repents and decides on a life of contrition and piety. After spending days planning his new career as a soldier of Christ, in the *Reminiscences* he tells us that he subsequently returned to his previous thoughts of pursuing and charming a certain noble lady whose identity has still not been discovered.[43] But this is now where the interesting thing happens, which will eventually lead in a straight line to the 'Rules for the Discernment of Spirits' in the *Spiritual Exercises* which would later influence St John of the Cross. For he noticed that his sexual thoughts of pursuing the lady in question would initially delight and stimulate him but would ultimately leave him feeling dry and dissatisfied, whereas his earlier thoughts of leading a life dedicated to Christ retained their joy long after he had thought about them. Thus, as he writes in the *Reminiscences*, 'little by little he came to recognise the difference between the spirits that were stirring him, one from the devil and the other from God'.[44] This is what he would later call the 'Discernment of Spirits'. Ignatius had felt the full force of the Tristan wound – the erotic wound at the centre of the soul – and yet had realized that ultimately it could only be healed by pursuing its origins to the transcendent centre of the self.

A QUESTION OF FEELING

What is probably most striking to the contemporary reader is the importance of feeling and affect in Ignatius's notion of 'discernment of the soul'. In his summary of these events later published as the *Spiritual Exercises* he returns frequently to the Spanish words *sentir* and *gustar*: literally to 'sense/feel' and 'enjoy/savour/taste'[45] the action of the Spirit of God in our lives. See, for example, Exx 2.3:

> Whether this comes from one's own reasoning or because the understanding is enlightened by the divine power, [the retreatant] will get more spiritual relish and fruit, than if the one who is giving the Exercises had much explained and amplified the meaning of the events. For it is not knowing much but deep down feeling and relishing things interiorly that contents and satisfies the soul.[46]

Like his later Spanish contemporaries Teresa of Avila and John of the Cross, Ignatius presents a 'full bodied' spirituality that wants to take in all aspects of the self, not just what we might call 'pious' or 'holy' feelings or sensations. His spirituality, then, must find 'God in all things'. For Ignatius, nothing is not worthy of study or investigation, especially in the human *psyche*, for nothing is beyond the reach of God's grace. In this respect Ignatius's *Exercises* lie in that tradition of psychological confession we encountered earlier in the desert; however, it is one that is harnessed to directing the gaze of the soul on to the transcendent.

It is this aspect of Ignatius's writing that John of the Cross so cherishes when he talks about 'discernment' or, as he terms it, *discreción*, in the spiritual director or confessor and realizes that this special commodity is at the heart of spiritual direction and confession.[47]

In an earlier chapter we contrasted the 'psychological' approach of the desert elders with the 'transcendent' approach of Augustine. The genius of John, as I see it, is in his ability to combine the two once again. Like Abhishiktananda, he is able to experience the move to the transcendental abyss beyond language, while having the ability to retain the 'psychological' verisimilitude necessary to navigate that transition. For, in contrast to so many of his fellow Christian theologians, John's theology starts not with a biblical pronouncement or church doctrine but with the stark psychological experience of the wound we experience at the heart of our existence:

> Where have you hidden,
> My love, and left me moaning?
> Like a stag you fled
> having wounded me;
> I went out calling you, and you had gone.
>
> And all who are free,
> Tell me a thousand graceful things of you;
> And all wound me more,
> and leave me dying:

A don't-know-what which lies behind their babbling.
Why, if you wounded this heart,
Don't you heal it?
And as you stole it from me,
Why do you leave it as it is
and not carry off what you have stolen?[48]

This strange and terrible cry at once makes John's theology so appealing and so unusual. His is a theology built not on abstract theories of divinity but rather on the ordinary flesh-and-blood lives of mortals. His own hard upbringing and the difficult circumstances of his life no doubt contributed to this – his father died when John was young, leaving his mother, disowned by her husband's family, to bring up the family in destitute straits (indeed, one of his brothers probably died of malnutrition).[49] Yet, from his own personal experience, John's meditations allow his own personal suffering to take on a universal relevance, for at the heart of his writing, deeply confessional in nature, is the sense, somehow, that God has left us, leaving us with a feeling of unease, dissatisfaction or failure. Somehow we are imperfect and what we seek cannot be found. This is indeed the 'holy wound' that lies at the heart of all human life with which we began this book. In this respect, then, the fact that John's theology starts with a confessional *cri de coeur* is no coincidence. He recognizes that *all true theology, all true examination of the divine, must start with the groan of the confessional*.

I am convinced, therefore, that one of the reasons for John's renewed appeal to our generation is that once again we are understanding that at the heart of the contemporary world there lies a deep, festering and painful spiritual wound – what I have called throughout this book the 'Tristan wound'. As we have seen, many contemporary commentators have discussed it – for example, Richard Rohr, Henri Nouwen and Robert Johnson.[50] Robert Johnson, for example, suggests that most Western people have this transcendent wound. In our youth, like the Lord Tristan, we encounter something beyond our ken and yet we cannot contain and hold the transcendent we encounter within our *psyches* – it literally blows our mind and can end up making us bitter towards all that is transcendent, especially organized religion, for the rest of our lives. Many of us, he argues, have 'blundered into something that is too big for them. They proceed halfway through their development and then drop it as being too hot. Often a certain bitterness arises, because ... they can neither live with the new consciousness they have touched nor can they entirely drop it.'[51] As Abbot Mark Patrick Hedermann puts it, 'whatever is thrown against eternity forever afterwards bears the mark of that bruising encounter'.[52]

So it is that four hundred years earlier we find John also beginning his theological journey with this deep spiritual wound:

This feeling is so strong because in the love-wound that God produces in the soul, the affection of the will rises with sudden rapidity toward the possession of the Beloved, whose touch was felt. Just as quickly, she feels his absence and the impossibility of possessing him here as she wants. And together with this feeling, she then experiences 'moaning' over his absence.[53]

From this wound arises John's first theological point as expressed in *The Spiritual Canticle*:

> It is noteworthy that, however elevated God's communications and the experiences of his presence are, and however sublime a person's knowledge of him may be, these are not God essentially, nor are they comparable to him because, indeed, he is still hidden to the soul. Hence, regardless of all these lofty experiences, a person should think of him as hidden and seek him as one who is hidden, saying: 'where have You hidden?'[54]

This 'hiddenness' of God, the *deus absconditus*, is a lodestone for much of John's theology. God will always be beyond our imaginings. We are again at the point where Abhishiktananda found himself by the banks of the Ganges – an encounter with a God beyond imaginings – beyond religion even. The transcendent wound, like the 'living flame of love', burns deeply and scalds the person who experiences it. Yet throughout John's account of 'the wound' there remains paradox – the 'happy wound' of the Easter liturgy that we mentioned earlier – and it is from this perspective that John offers his ointment for the healing of the transcendental wound. In the commentary on the third stanza of *The Living Flame of Love* he describes this as the need to 'excavate the caverns of the heart' to allow God's Holy Spirit to act in us. This process, often painful, is the basis of the Christian journey and the 'wound' on which everything else is predicated. It is the sublime wounding of the Spirit which touches us at the deepest centre, or *fondo del alma*. While this is happening we should remember, he writes, that 'if a person is seeking

God, his Beloved is seeking him much more'.[55] John's God, like Augustine's, is not one who stands aloof and indifferent to our spiritual suffering, but rather is one who will go out early, like the father of the Prodigal Son when 'he sees him far off', to come and rescue us. The basic human spiritual condition that John proposes is a dynamic one where we are running out to find God and God is running in to find us.

Therefore, when John talks of confession or spiritual direction he urges us to constantly remember that 'God is the principal agent in this matter'[56] who acts 'as a blind man's guide' to lead us to the 'place we know not'.[57] John always remembers that ultimately we cannot *know God in God's self*, in this life at least, and therefore there will always have to be a trust and letting go as we are led by God to that 'place we know not':

> God transcends the intellect and is incomprehensible and inaccessible to it. Hence while the intellect is understanding, it is not approaching God but withdrawing from him. It must withdraw from itself and from its knowledge so as to journey to God in faith, by believing and not understanding. In this way it reaches perfection, because it is joined to God by faith and not by any other means, and it reaches God more by not understanding than by understanding ... thus it advances by darkening itself, for faith is darkness to the intellect.[58]

This is the apophatic centre of the self that both Wittgenstein and Abhishiktananda describe in their own ways (and with which I concluded *The Pursuit of the Soul*). However, for John, the Christian response to this ongoing love of God is, as far as possible, not to put any blocks in the way of this outpouring love. The chief agent, says John, in spiritual direction and confession is the Holy Spirit, and all guides must never forget this,[59] avoiding putting obstacles in the way of God's action.

John was famous for his skills as a confessor, and as a young man he had honed his pastoral skills working with the sick and dying at the hospital for incurables, Nuestra Señora de la Concepción, at Medina del Campo. As is common in the tradition to which he is heir, he sees the one who confesses as 'putting on' the nature of their guide from constant meetings with them, so he attaches great importance to the quality and characteristics of the guide. The guide should be 'learned and discreet'[60] as well as having experience. Knowledge and discernment (*discreción*) are both important; however, he suggests, without 'experience of pure spirit' the guide will be useless. This immediately raises the bar regarding the suitability of a director and it is no surprise that he adds that the directee will rarely find 'a guide accomplished as to all their needs'.[61] 'God leads each one', he reminds us, 'along different paths so that hardly one spirit will be found like another in even half its method of procedure', which really should be written up in large letters on a board in front of anyone who practises the art of spiritual direction or confession. In spiritual guidance, he suggests, a certain slovenliness and apathy creeps in, a sort of sense that 'it has worked in the past so why shouldn't it work now?' In this respect John is always cognizant of the fact that confession is a 'mindless activity' where the intellect must often be suspended to enable the real action of the Spirit to work, what Freud would later call 'the gently hovering attention' of the good analyst. As the soul itself does not know what is happening, how, asks John, can the director or confessor possibly know?[62]

> Since (God) is the supernatural artificer, he will construct supernaturally in each soul the edifice he desires, if you, director, will prepare it by striving to annihilate it in its natural operations and affections, which have neither the ability nor strength to build the supernatural edifice. The natural operations and affections at this time impede rather than help. It is your duty to prepare the soul, and God's office, as the Wise Man says, is to direct its path, that is, toward supernatural goods, through modes and ways understandable to neither you nor the soul.[63]

The ultimate aim of the director or confessor, then, for John is to lead the soul to greater 'solitude, tranquility, and freedom of spirit'.[64] This latter quality, 'freedom of spirit', is very much at the heart of John's whole theology and teaching on confession:

> When the soul frees itself of all things and attains to emptiness and dispossession concerning them, which is equivalent to what it can do of itself, it is impossible that God fail to do his part by communicating himself to it, at least silently and secretly. It is more impossible than it would be for the sun not to shine on clear and uncluttered ground. As the sun rises in the morning and shines on your house so that its light may enter if you open the shutters, so God, who in watching over Israel does not doze or, still less, sleep, will enter the soul that is empty, and fill it with divine goods.[65]

So then, John advises, if we would be a confessor or spiritual director the first and last qualification is to 'know thyself'. If we are more proficient at guiding people at the more meditative stages then we should stick to that. Dangers arise when we go beyond our competencies and think that we know about spiritual things of which we have little knowledge and experience.[66]

JOHN AND DESIRE

We have seen in this chapter how John (following Ignatius of Loyola) builds upon the desert tradition presented earlier in this book to introduce a psychologically sophisticated approach to the question of individual confession – passing through the door to the transcendent while recognizing the abyss of the other to which Abhishiktananda's confessions gave powerful witness. I would like to end this chapter by introducing one final aspect of John's teaching which draws on this tradition: his understanding of 'the appetites'.

In considering John and the appetites, the first thing to take into account, as Chowning states, is that John's negation

> has nothing to do with neo-Platonic dualism or a denial of creation ... (He) is thoroughly Christian and incarnational. He exalts the beauty and dignity of creation and the purpose for which God created the world ... thus, creation reflects the presence, beauty and excellence of God and increases love in the person who reflects upon it.[67]

As a teacher and novice-master, John encouraged his students to find God in nature and the created order around. We saw above how Ignatius talked of 'God in all things', and his *Spiritual Exercises* ends with a remarkable 'Contemplation to Attain Love' where we read of the soul contemplating how:

> God dwells in creatures, in the elements, giving them being, in the plants allowing them to grow, in the animals feeding upon them, in people giving them to understand, and so in me, giving me being, animating me, giving me sensation and making me to understand (how) God works and labours for me in all things created on the face of the earth – that is, behaves like one who labours – as in the heavens, elements, plants, fruits, cattle etc., giving them being, preserving them, giving them growth and feeling.[68]

For both John and Ignatius, God is seen as being in all creation, and creation, as created by God, is very good indeed. Included in this is the human person, created in the image and likeness of God with all that that entails. In this respect both John and Ignatius have thoroughly absorbed St Thomas Aquinas in their university training in Salamanca and Paris respectively. Both show a true Thomist grasp of God's salvific action proceeding through 'grace building upon nature'. Therefore, our spiritual practices are not so much concerned with escaping matter and creation as they are with examining our own attitudes to nature and seeing how our craving and desire to seize matter is distorting our fundamental orientation as a being created in the image and likeness of God: 'John insists that what obstructs our relationship with God is not material reality as such, but the human heart when it craves, desires and tries to possess material objects, people and situations for selfish reasons.'[69]

Chapters 3–13 of *The Ascent of Mount Carmel* present John's deepest account of what he terms *los apetitos* – 'the appetites'. At first sight his definition of them seems largely negative:

> For the sake of a clearer and fuller understanding of our assertions, it will be beneficial to explain here how these appetites cause harm in two principal ways within those in whom they dwell: They deprive them of God's Spirit; and they weary, torment, darken, defile, and weaken them.[70]

> The appetites are wearisome and tiring because they agitate and disturb one just as wind disturbs water. And they so upset the soul that they do not let it rest in any place or thing.[71]

Yet to see John's anthropology of *los apetitos* as largely negative, as some commentators have done, is, I would argue, to miss out on the subtlety of his approach to human nature. The first distinction to draw is the difference John makes between what he terms 'natural' and 'voluntary' appetites. The former, he informs us, 'are little or no hindrance at all to the attainment of union',[72] for 'to eradicate the natural appetites, that is, to mortify them entirely, is impossible in this life'. Thus, as with the anthropology of the desert elders, to which we have seen John is heir, there is a basic substratum to our human nature that cannot be eradicated. This is akin to Jung's and Freud's postulate of 'the unconscious'. These passions are there and are to be seen as part of what makes us human. John never talks about eradicating the appetites, but always about redirecting them. This is not, as some commentators suggest, advocating destruction of the self, but *transformation* of the self. So, just as the natural appetites will remain and cannot do harm, the voluntary appetites, the consent to the natural appetites, will have to be redirected.

To help clarify this we could translate what John is attempting to describe here into contemporary psychological language. Here I am helped by a letter written in the 1960s by the British Benedictine Bede Griffiths, co-worker and friend of Henri Le Saux in India. Writing to a friend of his, Dr Mary Allen, a Jungian analyst who had helped financially to support his work in India, Bede Griffiths makes some startling analogies between the psychological insights of the twentieth century and the ancient Christian ascetic traditions of the desert elders. For Bede, the life of prayer is essentially a 'reordering' of the unconscious through the reflection of God's love: 'The point is that though these sins (pride, lust etc.) are largely unconscious: our <u>will</u> has consented to them. This is the mystery of original sin.' Much of the life of prayer, then, becomes for Bede a purification of the unconscious on this radical level: 'We are all by nature under the power of these forces of the unconscious ... these forces may be kept down, to some extent a kind of balance established, and that is the normal human condition, but it is very inadequate.'[73]

Struggling with the forces of the unconscious, we have two choices – to repress them or to give way to them in an undiscriminating fashion – 'becoming slaves to passion'. The first option, so common in the West, represses these forces so much that we become slaves to them in our efforts to control them: the power of repressing the libidinal forces uses up all our energy. As Bede Griffiths puts it: 'the average Christian simply represses the unconscious like everyone else and lives from their will and reason'. However, in baptism in Christ we have entered the deepest depths of the unconscious to allow their purification:

> It is Christ alone who can set us free from the unconscious. Baptism is a descent beneath the waters, a conflict with Satan (in which the soul is mystically identified with Christ) in which the daemonic powers are defeated and the healing powers of the unconscious are realised to give birth to new life.[74]

This, for Bede, is what should happen in our Christian life: 'the Holy Spirit should penetrate to the depth of the unconscious to the ultimate root of being, and transform us'. Thus, as with John, Bede advocates a descent into the deeper layers of unconscious motivation accompanied all the time by the spiritual presence of Christ, descending with us into the waters. Only by accepting the unconscious and surrendering it to the purifying action of the transcendent Spirit can we find the healing we are looking for.

As a practising psychotherapist I can attest to the truth of Bede's words in my encounters with clients. So many of us, especially in the West, lock up the forces of the unconscious and are terrified of opening up their contents (often with good reason); alternatively, we see around us total unconscious 'acting out' of the destructive unconscious forces of the *psyche*. For Bede, the life of Christ penetrating into the darkest depths of the unconscious can bring liberation and healing in a most unexpected and profound way. The goal, following Bede, is to bring about a marriage of the conscious and unconscious, the male and female, *animus* and *anima,* in which each is preserved and reintegrated in Christ. This is what John referred to earlier as the indwelling of the Blessed Trinity in the human *psyche* – the place of his 'fiestas'. Within this secret 'interior wine-cellar' the spiritual marriage of the self with the Divine will take place.

In contemporary terms, then, we can see John's 'natural appetites' as equivalent to the Freudian or Jungian 'unconscious', whereas the 'voluntary appetites' are equivalent to conscious choices arising out of deeper unconscious motivations. Such motivations are, for John, deeply embedded in the *psyche* and, no matter whether fine or gross, they can hinder spiritual progress:

> If one small crack in a pitcher goes unrepaired, the damage will be enough to cause all the liquid to leak out ... Accordingly, one imperfection leads to another, and these to still more. You will scarcely ever find a person negligent in the conquering of one appetite who will not have many others flowing from the identical weakness and imperfection caused by this one appetite. Such persons, consequently, are ever faltering along the road. We have witnessed many persons,

whom God was favoring with much progress in detach-
ment and freedom, fall from happiness and stability in
their spiritual exercises and end up losing everything
merely because they began to indulge in some slight
attachment to conversation and friendship under the
appearance of good. For by this attachment they gradually emptied themselves of both holy solitude and
the spirit and joy of God. All this happened because
they did not put a stop to their initial satisfaction and
sensitive pleasure, and preserve themselves for God in
solitude.[75]

This will be, then, the purpose of confession – to essay
those cracks and splits, to find the fissures in the *psyche*
through which the divine light of the transcendent can
shine. Which leads to John's famous list of exhortations
to 'the most difficult' which he illustrated on the map of
Mount Carmel he would draw for his penitents:

To reach satisfaction in all
desire satisfaction in nothing.
To come to possess all
desire the possession of nothing.
To arrive at being all
desire to be nothing.
To come to the knowledge of all
desire the knowledge of nothing.

To come to enjoy what you have not
you must go by a way in which you enjoy not.
To come to the knowledge you have not

you must go by a way in which you know not.
To come to the possession you have not
you must go by a way in which you possess not.
To come to be what you are not
you must go by a way in which you are not.[76]

Yet, as ever in his approach, John counsels two approaches to this steep and rugged path to perfection. First, that we should not despair in thinking about the path, but rather consider a practical approach to how these desires can be redirected. And second, that we take the same gentleness and pastoral sensitivity to the ascent which he himself took in his own dealings with penitents. Thus in *The Ascent* 1.13 he counsels four methods for 'redirection of the appetites', all of which shape his understanding of the role and purpose of confession.

The first is derived from the classic Thomist position described above. We must strive in all our actions and habits to 'imitate Christ' at all times. Thomas stresses that we should adopt the *habitus* of Christ, so that more and more in an unthinking (unconscious) fashion we adopt the ways and manner of living of Christ 'by bringing your life into conformity with his'.

Second, 'through love of Christ' we must renounce any sensory satisfaction that is 'not purely for the honour and glory of God'. The twentieth-century Jesuit and spiritual director Anthony de Mello, SJ, another co-worker of Abhishiktananda, suggested that at the end of the day before bed we should refrain from watching rubbish TV or reading trashy novels – today his counsel would probably also include avoiding the iPad or Facebook before bed.

As he says, if we put rubbish into the mind and soul we will get rubbish out.[77] Likewise, John suggests, we should choose to take in through our hearts and minds that which is conducive to creating greater peace and harmony in the self rather than exhaustion, fear and distraction.

This leads to the adoption of the next set of John's maxims for purification of the appetites:

Endeavor to be inclined always:
not to the easiest, but to the most difficult;
not to the most delightful, but to the most distasteful;
not to the most gratifying, but to the less pleasant;
not to what means rest for you, but to hard work;
not to the consoling, but to the unconsoling;
not to the most, but to the least;
not to the highest and most precious, but to the lowest and most despised;
not to wanting something, but to wanting nothing.
Do not go about looking for the best of temporal things, but for the worst, and, for Christ, desire to enter into complete nakedness, emptiness, and poverty in everything in the world.[78]

Yet, over and above his seemingly harsh counsel is John's gentle exhortation that the end to which we strive, the redirection of the appetites, will only be achieved through 'the other stronger love' that comes from God:

A love of pleasure, and attachment to it, usually fires the will toward the enjoyment of things that give pleasure. A more intense enkindling of another, better love (*otra inflamación mayor de otro amor major*), (love of the soul's Bridegroom), is necessary for the vanquishing of the appetites and the denial of this pleasure. By finding satisfaction and strength in this love, it will have the courage and constancy to readily deny all other appetites. The love of its Bridegroom is not the only requisite for conquering the strength of the sensitive appetites; an enkindling with urgent longings of love is also necessary. For the sensory appetites are moved and attracted toward sensory objects with such cravings that if the spiritual part of the soul is not fired with other, more urgent longings for spiritual things, the soul will be able neither to overcome the yoke of nature nor to enter the night of sense; nor will it have the courage to live in the darkness of all things by denying its appetites for them.[79]

John recognizes a profound insight here that only by this *otra inflamación mayor* can we be moved to tackle the steep and rough ascent of Mount Carmel which is the redirection of the appetites. We do not fight the will or the 'love of pleasure' (Freud's 'pleasure principle' – the essential libidinal nature of the soul); rather, we strive to cultivate the 'other, better love' which will ultimately lead our appetites back to their true home in God. Meditation, prayer and confession will lead to the redirection of our unconscious appetites – not to their annihilation.

To conclude, contrary to many popular misconceptions of John's doctrine, he does not disparage the things of the world; rather, he disparages our attitude to them. In as much as we are ensnared and enslaved (like a bird, he says, with its leg held by a thin wire, unable to fly), we will never be able to find the freedom we desire. A brush of the wing, he says, is necessary to remove these disordered appetites.

John's counsel of non-attachment is a counsel for redirection of the will, and by so doing, for a working on the deepest levels of unconscious desire and attachment – a reordering of self away from a centre of gravity based on the hungry ego and its insatiable demand but towards the eternal freedom and love that is life in peace with Christ. For John, negation is no end in itself, but rather it is a negation which arises from the 'other stronger love' of God. This, for John, and Ignatius, is the only process that will ultimately lead us to the 'place we know not': the place of the theological virtue of faith. From this point, found through confession, he offers the medicine for the healing of the wounded modern soul. As he would ultimately express it in his great poem, the *Dark Night of the Soul*:

> O guiding night!
> O night more lovely than the dawn!
> O night that has united
> the Lover with the beloved,
> transforming the beloved in the Lover.[80]

EPILOGUE

CONFESSION – THE HEALING
OF THE SOUL

We began our journey with the modern paradox of confession – a Cinderella sacrament that seems to be enjoying a new life shorn of its ecclesiastical robes and running free in its acquired secular garb. Along the way we have witnessed the rise of confessional practice as both a psychological art – the art of healing within the desert tradition – and a door to the transcendent as expounded by Augustine and adopted by the Western church. In the later medieval period we saw how confession moved into the confessional box and how its practices were codified as a sacrament of the Western church. Yet as the transcendental opportunity remained within the Church, the secular soul, wounded like Tristan on his bed, sought the transcendent through ultimately unsatisfying means such as the pursuit of romantic love with all its traps and ensnarements. Tristan, like us all, has the transcendent desire. The tragedy is that he places the desire in Isolde and so closes the door to the transcendent dimension to the soul. As Robert Johnson puts it: 'The incarnation symbolizes the synthesis (of body and soul); the love potion symbolizes the muddle. If we take our dual nature consciously we get to transcendent synthesis, if we take it haphazardly, we get the love potion.'¹ We late modern folk have also largely closed the door on to the transcendent, but, as we saw with Wittgenstein, the desire for it remains. It cannot be uprooted. Yet, like the philosopher, through the simple act of confession – whether on the analyst's couch, the chat-show sofa or the church pew – the door can creakingly be prised open once again.

As I have argued here, our three confessors – Ludwig Wittgenstein, Abhishiktananda and St John of the Cross – offer not only a way to rediscover the transcendent dimension but also a way that preserves the essential mystery of unknowing that lies at the heart of human personhood. As I suggested in my previous book, *The Pursuit of the Soul*, the Western soul lies sick with malaise. It seeks the transcendent but cannot find it. I have suggested in this book that the simple act of confession enables the healing of the soul. For, as I have argued, it is the means by which the soul may have its transcendental perspective restored.

We are today faced with a choice and are at a crossroads: either we take our transcendent nature seriously and thus allow healing into the soul, or we close ourselves to the possibility of the transcendent and so do untold psycho-logical damage to the self. By exposing ourselves to the scrutiny of another through the confessional process we are thus opening up the possibility of restoring wholeness to our being by restoring the transcendent perspective on the self and so answering our basic human need for fulfilment on all planes of existence. Confession is thus an archetypal act – once we express our own weakness, difficulty and failure to another we can allow the heal-ing process to begin. Modern psychology teaches us that

that healing will normally come from the most unlikely of places – whether it lies in the Norway, India or Ireland of the soul, the place where we least expected it will contain the sources of healing. In this respect, the Catholic liturgical sacrament of confession – a hybrid creature of transcendental and psychological structure – gives the possibility, through its liturgical symbolism, to effect in the one who confesses the reality which it represents. We might even say that Catholic sacramental confession is the archetypal confessional act *par excellence*. As Pope Francis, a great advocate of sacramental confession, puts it:

> It's true that there is always a certain amount of judge-ment in confession, but there is something greater than judgement that comes into play. It is being face-to-face with someone who acts *in persona Christi* to welcome and forgive you. It is an encounter with mercy.[2]

By putting open access to confession at the heart of his 'Year of Mercy' in 2016 the Pope acknowledged the force of the sacrament to reopen paths of healing within the postmodern soul. In the words of an old grandmother he encountered in Buenos Aires which he is fond of quoting: 'without mercy, without God's forgiveness, the world would not exist'.[3] He describes confession as the process of finding a crack, a tiny opening in a locked door, so that forgiveness and mercy can enter. For him, confession is not about 'cleaning the slate' but, as I have maintained throughout this book, about treating and healing a wound. In our case, the transcendent wound of the postmodern soul. In popularizing and reinvigorating the dialogue on confession, the Pope has opened up the possibility that the Cinderella sacrament may once again come in from the cold. For, by following the sacramental art, we will, as St Thomas Aquinas and St John of the Cross suggest, eventually become what we act out in the darkened box. Abbot Mark Patrick Hedermann of Glenstal Abbey in Ireland describes that liturgy as 'the enactment of the mystery of personhood'.[4] If we accept, as I have argued in this book, that at the heart of the human person lies the transcendent mystery, then the liturgical act of sacramental confession becomes the acting out in a liturgical setting, as Hedermann suggests, of the ultimate mystery of our existence as human beings:

> We celebrate what we become, now, at this moment, and forever afterwards ... it is something we step into like a new element, which we allow to encircle and to penetrate until we become saturated like seaweed ... eventually (it) takes over as the alternative energy running our lives.[5]

From this transcendental perspective, false confession – that is so often encountered – is a desire for a 'clean slate', the removal of sins so that I can go back to what I was doing before with very little change. From the transcendent (and indeed liturgical) perspective, true confession becomes the encounter with the person we really are in the abyss of silence and fire that lies so close to the sources of human life. As Søren Kierkegaard, the tormented Danish genius, put it so well in his *Purity of Heart*, which is a preparation, as he called it, for 'the office of Confession':

The purpose of the office of Confession is certainly not to make a man conscious of himself as an individual at the moment of its celebration, and then for the rest of time to allow him to live outside this consciousness ... For confession is a holy act, which calls for a collected mind. A collected mind is a mind that has collected itself from every distraction, from every relation, in order to centre itself upon this relation to itself as an individual who is responsible to God.[6]

The spiritual self is crucified daily in the midst of everyday cares, worries and failures. Confession is the means by which we are restored to our birthright – the abyss of love from which we were created.

ACKNOWLEDGEMENTS

Once again I would like to thank and acknowledge all those who have had confidence in this enterprise and encouraged me throughout its journey to fruition. Bloomsbury have been their usual outstandingly professional and kind selves in getting this manuscript ready for publication and I would in particular like to thank Jamie Birkett and Nick Fawcett for their help. Robin Baird-Smith has been as professional and committed an editor as one could hope to find, and without his constant help and guidance this book would not have come into existence. My colleagues and students at St Mary's University have helped me in so many ways. I particularly thank Dr Maureen Glackin and Dr Francis Campbell for supporting the writing process. Colleagues and friends from other institutions have been immensely supportive. For help in obtaining permissions and looking over drafts of the manuscript I would like to thank especially Professor Kevin Alban O. Carm., Professor Gavin D'Costa, Dr Mary Eaton, Fr Richard Finn, OP, Fr Iain Matthew, OCD, Professor Bernard McGinn, Professor Ray Monk, Dr Tarcisius Mukuka, Fr Richard Ounsworth, OP, Fr Kurian Perumpallikunnel, CMI and Hymie Wyse. Warm acknowledgement is also given to devoted family and friends, in particular Br Patrick Moore, Julienne McLean, Allyson Davies and Dr Ashish Deved. I thank the Dominican Council of the Order of Preachers of Great Britain for permission to use extracts from the correspondence of Fr Conrad Pepler, OP, and Louise Grosart and all at the Random House Archives for giving me access to his correspondence. 'Romanesque Arches' by Tomas Tranströmer is reproduced with the kind permission of Bloodaxe Books. As in my previous books, I thank all spiritual pilgrims and therapeutic clients for all they have taught me. And finally, I dedicate the book to my first confessor, Archbishop Kevin McDonald, who as a young curate had the unenviable task of hearing my first confession in a small parish in Worcestershire. It has been a great delight to renew our acquaintance in recent years and share his fascinating pastoral, ecumenical and faith-filled reflections once again — *ad multos annos!*

London
Easter, 2017

NOTES

INTRODUCTION

1 In *New Collected Poems*, 2011: 158.
2 1 Jn 3.20.
3 http://www.oprah.com//omagazine//your-guide-to
   -confessing-your-deep-dark-secrets.
4 Throughout I shall use the terms 'psyche' and 'soul' inter-
   changeably. For my reasoning behind this, please see my
   previous *The Pursuit of the Soul: Psychoanalysis, Soul-making and
   the Christian Tradition* (2016).
5 Berggren 1975: 1.
6 Taylor 2010: 65.

CHAPTER ONE

1 Freud/Breuer 1955: 68.
2 Freud 1959: 174.
3 Translated as 'Problems of Modern Psychotherapy', in Jung
   (1933) and CW: *The Practice of Psychotherapy*, 16. For full
   bibliographical references for all work by Freud and Jung, see
   the Bibliography.
4 Jung 1933: 35.
5 Jung 1933: 35.
6 Foucault 1998: 1.59.
7 Foucault 1998: 1.59.
8 Foucault 1998: 1.63.
9 Mk 1.15.
10 E.g. Mt. 3.2, 4.7, Lk. 5.32, 16.30, 24.47.
11 For more on the psychological and metaphysical nuances
   of the Greek term *nous*, I refer the reader to Tyler 2016,
   Chapters 2 and 3.

12   Kittel 1967: 977–9.
13   See Kittel 1967: 989–90.
14   Joel 1–2.
15   Hos. 7.
16   Jon. 3.
17   Joel 1.13-14.
18   Isa. 58.6-8.
19   Joel 2.12-13.
20   Lk. 16.19-31.
21   2 Cor. 13.5; see *The Life of St Anthony*: 55.
22   *Sayings of the Desert Fathers* in Ward 1984: 13.
23   *Conferences* 2.16.1.
24   *Conferences* 2.10.1.
25   *Conferences* 2.10.1.
26   *Conferences* 2.11.4.
27   *Conferences* 2.8.1.
28   *Conferences* 2.13.1.
29   Abba Moses in Cassian *Conferences* 2.10.1.
30   *Conferences* 9.5.1.
31   *Conferences* 9.6.4.
32   *Praktikos*: 13.
33   *Conferences* 2.13.7.
34   *Conferences* 2.8.9.
35   Although, as Dallen points out (1991: 105), the Eastern
     tradition would later link the reconciliation and practice of
     penance to liturgical offices in a communal setting. Celtic
     monasticism, he suggests, 'seems to have copied the Eastern
     monastic practice at an early stage of its development before
     it had advanced beyond simple spiritual direction and been
     integrated within the monastic liturgy'.
36   See Ware 1982: 38.
37   *Ladder of Ascent*: 5, p. 130.
38   Ware 1982: 38.
39   Ware 1982: 39.
40   McGinn (1991: 232) nicely summarizes the situation regard-
     ing the secondary commentary on Augustine: 'Concerning
     Augustine there are few new debates and perhaps even

fewer cases of scholarly consensus in disputed areas.' Here I shall use the Latin version of the *Confessions* and commentary in O'Donnell 1992 and the English translation of Sheed 2006 with modifications as necessary; for all other works of Augustine cited, see the bibliography.

41 For more on these influences, see Tyler 2016.

42 *Confessions* 4.4.9.

43 *Retractions* 32.

44 O'Donnell 1992: 2:3.

45 See O'Donnell 1992 2:3–7.

46 See McGinn 2016: 41.

47 Hom Ps.: 313, Exposition 2 of Ps. 29: 19.

48 See O'Donnell 1992: 2.4 and McGinn 2016. Following McGinn, for *confessio veritatis* – the confession of truth – see *Conf*: 5.6.11, 8.10.24, 11.7.9, as well as five texts in Book 12 (*Conf*: 12.3.3, 12.10.10, 12.18.27, 12.23.32 and 12.25.35). The term *confessio fidei* is found in Book 13.14.15 (as a baptismal formula) and *confessio ignorantiae* – the confession of ignorance – is to be found in *Conf*: 11.22.28, 11.25.32, 12.6.6 and 12.30.41.

49 McGinn 2016: 42.

50 McGinn 2016: 37.

51 McGinn 2016: 38.

52 *Confessions* 10.17.1.

53 *Confessions* 10.17.

54 *Confessions* 10.17.

55 *Confessions* 10.5.7.

56 Trapè 1986: 454.

57 Comm Gen: 3.20.30, see also Trin: 14.25.

58 Books 9–15 of *On the Trinity*. Bernard McGinn in a number of articles has drawn attention to the difference between 'likeness' (*similitudo*) and 'image' (*imago*) of the soul to God in Augustine's writings. For more, see McGinn 1991: 243/44, and 2010.

59 Jn 14.6.

60 See also *Confessions* 7.18.24.

61 Hom Ps.: 52.6: '*Filius enim Dei particeps mortalitatis effectus est, ut mortalis homo fiat particeps diuinitatis.*'

62 Hom Ps.: 49.1.2: '*Manifestum est ergo, quia hominess dixit deos, ex gratia sua deificatos, no de substantia sua natos ... et ille deificat qui per seipsum non alterius participation Deus est.*'

63 *Confessions* 1.6.

64 *Confessions* 10.1.1.

65 O'Donnell 1992: 1.xvii.

CHAPTER TWO

1   Adapted from the *Tristan* of Bédier, 1913: 13.

2   Mt. 16.19.

3   Mt. 18.22.

4   Rahner 1969: 389.

5   *The Rule of Community* 1 QS, VI, 25–VII, 25.

6   Mk. 2.10.

7   *On Penitence*: 10.

8   *On Penitence*: 40, cf. 1 Tim. 1.19 and Plato, *Phaedo* 85d.

9   Rahner 1983: 11.

10 Rahner 1969: 392.

11 Dallen 1991: 76.

12 Within a generation of Augustine's death St Patrick will write an influential *confessio*, thus attesting to the early love of the form in the Celtic lands. I am indebted to Bernard McGinn to drawing this to my attention.

13 Dallen 1991: 103.

14 Dallen 1991: 103.

15 See Rahner 1969: 394.

16 Rahner 1983: 14.

17 ST: Qu. 84, art. 1.

18 ST: Qu. 84, art. 10.

19 ST: Qu. 68, art. 6.

20 Dallen 1991: 142.

21 See Tyler 2016.

22 *Philosophical Investigations*: 124. For more on the relationship between Wittgenstein's philosophy and Christian spirituality, see Tyler 2011.

23 *Philosophical Investigations*: 126.

24 Wittgenstein uses the phrase *Übersichtlichkeit* – literally, 'right seeing' or 'clear overview'; however, he did also use the English translation 'overlook' for the concept. For an excellent recent discussion on Wittgenstein's choreography of saying and showing in relation to his views of self, see Chapter Two of Jose Nandhikkara's *Being Human after Wittgenstein* (Nandhikkara 2011).

25 *Philosophical Investigations*: 309.

26 Johnson 1996: 78.

27 VB: 459. Written as a draft foreword to *Philosophische Bemerkungen* in 1930. See also *Zettel* 464: 'The pedigree of psychological phenomena: I strive not for exactitude but a clear over-view.'

28 The German word for 'unconscious' is *das Unbewusst*, literally 'the unknown thing'.

29 Johnson 1996: 13.

30 See Tyler 2016.

31 Tagore 1961: 358.

32 *The Tristan Legend of Gottfried of Strassburg* 1: 1995–2000, Hatto: 67. I have used the original Middle High German/New High German version in Ranke's edition together with Hatto's translation into English, which I have adjusted as necessary. For more information on these editions, see the Bibliography.

33 Johnson 1987: 16–17.

34 Johnson 1987: 17.

35 Johnson 1987: 21.

36 *LS*: 18.

37 *LS*: 19.

38 *LS*: 54.

39 *LS*: 85.

40 *LS* 32–4.

41 *Tristan*: 2075–80.

42 '*In seiner ersten Freiheit, wurde all seine Freiheit vernichtet.*' *Tristan*: 1.133, 2075–80.

43 *Tristan*, Hatto: 69

44 Johnson 1987: 25.

45 See Tyler 2013.

46 *Tristan*, Hatto: 71.

47 *Tristan*, Hatto: 133.

48 *Tristan*, Hatto: 138.

49 *Tristan*, Bédier: 13.

50 Rohr 1996: 85–6.

51 Rohr 1996: 85–6.

52 Rohr 1996: 85–6.

53 1996: 87

54 RFGB, p. 199.

55 Rohr 1996: 89.

56 See, for example, de Rougemont 1963, 1983.

CHAPTER THREE

1   BTS: 407, PO: 161/2.

2   Monk 1990: 94.

3   Monk 1990: 94.

4   Letter to Russell, December 1913 or January 1914, in LR: 57. See Monk 1990: 596 and McGuinness 1988: 192 on the disputed dating of this letter. I have substituted 'put my house in order' for '*muss ich mit mir selbst in's Reihe kommen!*' For references to Wittgenstein's work used, see the bibliography.

5   Russell to Wittgenstein's sister Hermine, quoted in Rhees 1987: 2.

6   LW to BR, 15 December 1913, in LR: 45.

7   LW to BR, January 1914, LR: 46/7.

8   LW to BR, 3 March 1914, LR: 52/3.

9   Russell to Lady Ottoline Morrell, 19 February 1914, in Monk 1990: 99.

10 LW to BR, December 1913/January 1914, LR: 57/8.

11 NB: 4 May 1916.

12 McGuinness 1988: 242.

13 BEE: 27 April 1916. This and later quotes from his personal diaries are taken from the Bergen Electronic Edition of Wittgenstein's *Nachlass* with my own translation: '*So bin ich jetzt fast immer umgeben von Leuten, die mich hassen. Und dies ist*

das Einziges, womit ich mich noch nicht abfinden kann. Hier sind
aber böse, herzlose Menschen. Es ist mir fast unmöglich, eien Spur
von Menschlichkeit in ihnen zu finden. Gott helfe mir zu leben …
Gott sei mit mir! Amen.'

14   BEE: 8 May 1916. 103 10v: '*Die Leute, mit denen ich beisammen*
bin, sind nicht so sehr gemein, als <u>ungeheuer</u> beschränkt. Das macht
den Verkehr mit ihnen fast unmöglich, weil sie einen ewig missverste-
hen. Die Leute sind nicht dumm, aber beschränkt. Sie sind in ihrem
Kreise klug genug. Aber es fehlt ihnen der Charakter und damit die
Ausdehnung."Alles versteht das rechtgläubige Herz".'

15   McGuinness 1988: 245.

16   NB: 2 August 1916.

17   See Tyler 2011.

18   BR to OM, 20 December 1919, in LR: 82.

19   Monk 1990: 115.

20   Rhees 1987: 3.

21   Letter from Russell to Lady Ottoline Morrell, 20 December
      1919, in LR: 82.

22   Letter from Wittgenstein to Ludwig Ficker, LF: 24 July 1915.

23   BEE 5 September 1914, 103 10v: '*Ich bin auf dem Wege zu einer*
grossen Entdeckung. Aber ob ich danhingelangen werde?!'

24   Monk 1990: 117.

25   Sontag 2000.

26   LPE: 109.

27   Tolstoy 1895: xv.

28   Tolstoy 1895: xvi.

29   See LPE: 80.

30   Tolstoy 1904: 8.

31   Tolstoy 1904: 9.

32   Tolstoy 1904: 16.

33   Tolstoy 1904: 19–20.

34   Tolstoy 1904: 26.

35   Tolstoy 1904: 59.

36   Tolstoy 1904: 66.

37   Tolstoy 1904: 79.

38   Tolstoy 1904: 69.

39   LPE: 78.

40   Conversation with Franz Parak recorded in Monk 1990: 159.
'He seriously contemplates becoming a monk': Bertrand
Russell to Lady Ottoline Morrell, 20 December 1919, in
LR: 82.

41   Monk 1990: 170.

42   PE to LW, 19 June 1920, in Monk 1990: 186.

43   LW to PE, 21 June 1920, LPE: 32.

44   JMK to LL, 18 January 1929, in Monk 1990: 255.

45   This was to be Wittgenstein's longest stay in Norway, lasting
(with two small interruptions) until December 1937. During
this time he stayed for long periods on his own in the chalet
he had had constructed on the banks of Lake Eidsvatnet near
the Sogne mountains. The chalet was built to his own design
but later taken down after his death and reconstructed in the
village of Skjolden; however, to this day, the place the hut had
occupied is still referred to by villagers as 'Little Austria'.
For more information on the practical arrangements of
Wittgenstein's stay in Norway, see Johannessen, Larsen and
Åmås, 1994.

46   RFGB: 118.

47   Monk 1990: 367.

48   RFGB: 118.

49   '*Cum ipsi (majores homines) appellabant rem aliquam, et cum secun-
dum earn vocem corpus ad aliquid movebant, videbam, et tenebam hoc
ab eis vocari rem illam, quod sonabant, cum earn vellent ostendere.
Hoc autem eos veile ex motu corporis aperiebatur: tamquam verbis
naturalibus omnium gentium, quae fiunt vultu et nutu oculorum,
ceterorumque membrorum actu, et sonitu vocis indicante affectionem
animi in petendis, habendis, rejiciendis, fugiendisve rebus. Ita verba in
variis sententiis locis suis posita, et crebro audita, quarum rerum signa
essent, paulatim colligebam, measque jam voluntates, edomito in eis
signis ore, per haec enuntiabam.*' (Augustine, *Confessions*: 1. 8)

50   Monk 1990: 366.

51   LPE: xiv.

52   CV: preface.

53   Klagge 2001.

54   Hereafter GT.

55 Ludwig Hänsel, 1886–1959, an Austrian friend and confidant of Wittgenstein whom he had met at the prisoner of war camp in Cassino at the end of the First World War.

56 PPO: 151.

57 PPO: 151.

58 VB: 1937.

59 PPO: 153.

60 LW to LH, 7 November 1936, in PPO: 281.

61 PPO: 283.

62 Monk 1990: 361–84.

63 PPO: 151.

64 FB: 154.

65 Monk 1990: 368.

66 Rhees 1987: 35.

67 PPO: 157, GT: 27 January 1937.

68 FS to LW, 6 December 1936, in Monk 1990: 367.

69 FS to LW, 9 December 1936, in Monk 1990: 368.

70 PPO: 155.

71 PPO: 183.

72 PPO: 221.

73 BT.

74 BTS: 407, PO: 161/2.

75 BTS: 406, PO: 160.

76 Rhees 1987: 37.

77 Monk 1990: 370/1.

78 Monk 1990: 371.

79 See Monk 1990: 371.

80 RFGB: 118.

81 Rhees 1987: 173.

82 See Cavell 1991: 72: 'his writing is deeply practical and negative, the way Freud's is. And like Freud's therapy, it wishes to prevent understanding which is unaccompanied by inner change.'

83 LC: 41–52.

84 LC: 45–6.

85 PI: 309.

86 LPE: 143.

87 T: 4.1212.

88 See Tyler 2016, Chapter 7.

89 See Cavell 1976, 1979.

90 Crary and Read 2000.

91 Hosseini 2007; see, too, Nandhikkara 2011, which takes a similarly humanistic approach.

92 See Kerr 1997 for a good analysis of this.

93 VB: 1946.

94 PPO: 172.

95 PPO: 173.

96 LPE: 98.

97 PI: 107. The paragraph recalls Wittgenstein's walk to the local village in Norway for supplies when his lake froze in the winter months and the rowing boat became useless.

98 PI: 97.

99 LW to NM, 16 November 1944, in Malcolm 2001: 93.

100 VB: 1931.

101 Rhees 1987: 95.

102 Rhees 1987: 79.

103 Unpublished letter to Ray Monk, 10 September 1986.

104 GT: 175.

105 LPE: 97.

106 BEE: 103: 29 March 1916: '*Jetzt Inspektion. Meine Seele schrumpft zusammen. Gott erleuchte mir! Gott erleuchte meine Seele!*'

107 BEE: 103: 30 March 1916: '*Tu dein Bestes! Mehr kannst du nicht tun: und sei heiter ... Hilf dir selbst und hilf anderen mit deiner ganzen Kraft. Und dabei sei heiter! Aber wieviel Kraft soll man für sich, und wieviel für die anderen brauchen? Schwer ist es, gut zu leben!! Aber das gute Leben ist schön. Aber nicht mein, sondern Dein Wille geschehe!*'

108 BEE 103: '*Gewiss, das Christentum ist der einzige sichere Weg zum Glück. Aber wie, wenn einer dies Glück verschmähte?! Könnte es nicht besser sein, unglücklich, im hoffnungslosen Kampf gegen die äussere Welt augrunde zu gehen? Aber ein solches Leben ist sinnlos. Aber warum nicht ein sinnloses Leben führen? Ist es unwürdig?*'

109 Diary 27 January 1937, PPO: 157.

110 PPO: 163.

111 PPO: 169.

112 BEE: 15 February 1937, 183: 168: '*Wie das Insekt das Licht umschwirrt so ich ums Neue Testament.*'

113 BEE: 16 February 1937, 183: 202: '*Gott! Lass mich zu dir in ein Verhältnis kommen, in dem ich fröhlich sein kann in meiner Arbeit! <u>Glaube</u> daran dass Gott von Dir in jedem Moment <u>alles</u> fordern kann! Sei Dir dessen wirklich bewusst! Dann bitte dass er Dir das Geschenk des Lebens gibt!*'

114 PPO: 175.

115 PPO: 183, 17 February 1937.

116 PPO: 191, 18 February 1937. See also his letter to Engelmann, 21 June 1920, LPE: 35: 'of course it all boils down to the fact that I have no faith!' followed by the enigmatic statement, 'Well, we shall see!' (*Nun wir werden sehen!*)

117 PPO: 193, 19 February 1937.

118 PPO: 195, 19 February 1937.

119 PPO: 197, 20 February 1937.

120 PPO: 199, 20 February 1937.

121 Or 'metaphor'. Wittgenstein seems close in his use here to the final chorus of Goethe's *Faust*: '*Alles vergängliche ist nur ein Gleichnis …*' ('Everything fleeting is but a likeness …').

122 PPO: 181.

123 T: 7.

124 CV: 1937.

125 PPO: 205, 22 February 1937.

CHAPTER FOUR

1 Description of an encounter with Swami Abhishiktananda a year before his death given by Kenneth Sharpe in July 1972. Originally published in the *North Indian Churchman* and quoted in Letters: 266. For full details of the work of Abhishiktananda quotes and abbreviations, see the bibliography.

2 Born in 1910 to a poor Breton family, Henri Le Saux had a long interest in India and Indian spirituality. At an early age he joined the minor seminary at Châteaugiron in 1921

before entering the Benedictine order at the Abbey of Sainte-Anne de Kergonan in 1929. In 1948 he sailed to India to begin a monastic community with his fellow French priest, Jules Monchanin, their aim being to live the ancient Western monastic life within the frame and ambit of classical Indian ideas, philosophy and spiritual practice. The monastery they founded, normally called Shantivanam (The Forest of Peace), survived their passing and today flourishes; however, while they both lived there it largely remained (as both priests liked it) a quiet and empty hermitage. Both priests began wearing the *kavi* of the Indian renouncer in the 1950s, at which time Henri Le Saux took the name Abishikteśvarānda (here I have used the normal English version of his name, Swami Abhishiktananda, omitting the diacritics). In 1968, Abhishiktananda decided to head north to the source of the Ganges, where he spent the final years of his life alternating between a small hermitage he had built there and seeking to convey his message to a new generation of seekers in India.

3   Le Saux attracted many sobriquets and epithets while in India, including Swamiji.

4   Diary: xiii.

5   Panikkar follows this line in entitling the published diary 'The Ascent to the Depth of the Heart'. The original source of the phrase for Swamiji is a French translation of an Upanishad dedicated to Ramana Maharshi: '*au sein du fond, au coeur d'Arunachal*'. The phrase '*au sein du fond*' was a translation of '*hridayakuh aram adhye*', in *Sri Ramana Gita II*. See Diary: 81, fn. 59.

6   Diary: xiv.

7   Diary: xvi.

8   Diary: xvi.

9   Diary: 28.

10   Diary: 28, 31 March 1952.

11   Letters: 28.

12   See Du Boulay 2005: 69.

13   I take this working definition of *advaita* from Panikkar's *Opera Omnia*, Volume 1: 'nondualism (*a-dvaita*). Spiritual intuition

that sees ultimate reality as neither monistic nor dualistic. The recognition that the merely quantitative problem of the one and the many in dialectical reasoning does not apply to the realm of ultimate reality. The latter, in fact, possesses polarities that cannot be divided into multiple separate units; not to be confused with *monism*' (Panikkar 2014: 331).

14 The name Arunāchala, literally 'the rosy one', refers to the beauty of the mountain in the early dawn light. It had become in Tamil lore a watchword for enlightenment and awakening. Dedicated to Lord Shiva, it is near the town of Tiruvannāmalai in Tamil Nadu.

15 Secret: 5–6. *The Secret of Arunāchala* (hereafter *Secret*) was one of the few autobiographical accounts that Swamiji prepared for open publication. Many of its passages are directly taken from the *Spiritual Diary*.

16 *Darśana*, literally 'a seeing', has in the Sanskrit tradition the nuances of seeing, blessing and benediction.

17 Secret: 14.

18 *Mahānārāyana Upanishad* 12: 14.

19 Letters: 31.

20 Diary: 61, 7 March 1953.

21 Diary: 163, 15 November 1956.

22 Letters: 242, 23 December 1970.

23 Letters: 218, 24 August 1969.

24 E.g., see Diary: 31, 3 April 1952 and 310, 23 March 1970.

25 Diary: 85.

26 Diary: 310, 23 March 1970.

27 Diary: 336, 24 December 1971.

28 Williams 1990: 3.

29 Panikkar 1973: 44.

30 Panikkar 1973: 33.

31 Panikkar 1973: 33

32 Panikkar 1973: 54.

33 Panikkar 1973: 550. Panikkar's insight to base his interfaith encounter within the Trinitarian structure of Christianity is one that is taken up by both Archbishop Rowan Williams and Professor Gavin D'Costa in the volume cited earlier

(D'Costa 1990) and that still continues to influence contemporary interfaith dialogue from a Christian perspective. In the words of Williams: 'The language of the first Christian theologians, Paul and John above all, assumes that *Christ* is a word that has come to mark out the shape of the potential future of all human beings, while remaining at the same time the designation of a specific person. The event of Jesus' life, death and resurrection is not (or not only) an external model to be imitated. The important thing about it is that it has created a different sort of human community; professing commitment to Jesus as Lord connects us not only to Jesus but to one another in a new way' (Williams 1990: 7). For D'Costa the 'exclusivist emphasis on the particularity of Christ and the pluralist emphasis on God's universal activity in history' are especially reconciled through the individual acts of 'serving God and neighbour and living the Good News' by Christ's followers today in his living community, the Church (D'Costa 1990: 26–7).

34 Diary: xiii.
35 'Méta-théologie et théologie diacritique', in *Concilium*, 46, 1969.
36 Letters: 217, 10 July 1969.
37 Letters: 244, 26 January 1971.
38 Letters: 217.
39 *Abhishiktānanda's Non-Monistic Advaitic Experience*, by John Glenn Friesen, PhD thesis, University of South Africa, 2001.
40 Diary: 32.
41 Friesen 2001: 410.
42 Friesen 2001: 411, 418.
43 Abhishiktananda himself refers to this position in a diary entry of 5 July 1956 as '*an-advaita*'.
44 Letters: 209.
45 Diary: 388, 12 September 1973.
46 Letters: 215, 26 July 1969.
47 Letters: 267, 22 May 1972.
48 Letter to Murray Rogers, 2 September 1973, Letters: 310.
49 Letter to Marc Chaduc, 21 January 1973, Letters: 284.

50   Diary: 117, 26 August 1955.

51   Diary: 126, 15 September 1955.

52   Diary: 148, 21 March 1956.

53   Diary: 203, 12 April 1957.

54   Diary: 1958, Du Boulay 2005: 165.

55   Letter to Ann-Marie Stokes, 9 February 1967, Letters: 190.

56   Letter to Ann-Marie Stokes, 9 February 1967, Letters: 190.

57   Letters: 171–2.

58   *Sagesse Hindoue, Mystique Chrétienne*, published in English as *Saccidānanda: A Christian Approach to Advaitic Experience* by ISPCK in 1974.

59   See Letters: 221 and 223 to Panikkar, 29 October 1969 and 11 December 1969; also Diary: 33, 4 April 1952.

60   Chryssavgis 2003: 45–6.

61   Letters: 229, 4 March 1970.

62   Letters: 228.

63   Letters: 229.

64   Letter to Panikkar, 5 December 1969, Letters: 223.

65   Letter to Panikkar, 11 December 1969, Letters: 223.

66   Letter to Marc Chaduc, 21 January 1973, Letters: 284.

67   Diary: 34, 4 April 1952.

68   Diary: 33, 4 April 1952.

69   Diary: 88, 7 January 1954.

70   Diary: 88, 7 January 1954.

71   See Thottakara 2009 and Tagore 1996.

72   Friesen suggests that at this point Abhishiktananda is more Buddhist than Hindu in his understanding of *sannyāsa* – perhaps influenced by his reading of Alan Watts; see Friesen 2001: 271. To support this view, see Diary: 70, 30 March 1953: 'I have understood silence – and also what is beyond silence, emptiness (*sunyata*).'

73   Diary: 88, 7 January 1954.

74   Sann: 18.

75   Sann: 22.

76   Sann: 22.

77   Letter to Marc Chaduc, 8 April 1973, Letters: 293.

78   See Du Boulay 2005: 229–30. The mystery of the

disappearance of Marc has never been resolved. To this day various theories abound, including the possibility of a ritual suicide, murder or that he may even still be alive.

79   Du Boulay 2005: 230.

80   From the Sanskrit *jñana* – the path of wisdom, as opposed to the path of devotion (*bhakti*) or action (*karma*).

81   Dr Cuttat to Ilse Friedeberg and Murray Rogers, 8 July 1972, the Murray Rogers Collection, quoted in Du Boulay 2005: 184.

82   Diary: 136, 6 January 1956.

83   Commentators such as D'Costa (in publicly written texts and private correspondence) have rightly pointed out the extreme individualism of much of Abhishiktananda's approach; this cannot be denied. As with Wittgenstein's approach to philosophy, this has drawbacks and advantages. The drawback for both philosopher and monk is that it will be difficult for their discourse to be neatly categorized within the ongoing dialogue of the respective disciplines of academic philosophy and theology. However, from a pastoral perspective, and here the value of the confessional comes to the fore, their private confessions allow us insights into the malaise of the contemporary soul and how this might be healed. This is the path I follow here; however, I hope to return to some of these questions of interpretation in a later work.

84   Diary: 342, 8 April 1972.

85   Letters: 286, 4 February 1973.

86   Diary: 81, 10–20 December 1953.

87   Letter to Sr Thérèse de Jésus, 16 January 1973, Letters: 283. See also Diary, 22 May 1972: 'It is too much to feel yourself in the presence of the Truth – it scorches you!' and Diary: 154, 6 August 1956: 'it is a terrible thing to fall into the hands of the living God (Hebrews 10:31) ... The living *Saccidānanda* is a devouring fire.'

88   Letters: 306.

89   Letter to Sr Marie Thérèse Le Saux, 9 August 1973, Letters: 308.

90   Letter to Odette Baumer-Despeigne, 4 September 1973, Letters: 312. I concluded the first part of this trilogy, *The*

Pursuit of the Soul, by suggesting that the soul is best described in terms of embodiment, paradox, ambiguity and the symbolic. The breakthrough of the symbolic and the poetic in the writings of Abhishiktananda and in those of St John of the Cross, which we shall examine in the final chapter, underscores the value of this approach.

91   Diary: 386, 11 September 1973.

92   See Diary: 387.

93   See Diary: 43/44, 8 June 1952: 'There is in us no enjoyment which does not have its source at the core of our being in the divine *ānandam*, the joy that God takes in himself, and there-fore in us … and there is in us no action, however ordinary it may seem, which is not derived from and identified with the divine play (*līlā*) and the divine *līlā* is nothing else than God.'

94   Letter to Marc Chaduc, 26 January 1973, Letters: 285.

95   Diary: 261, 24 September 1963.

CHAPTER FIVE

1   St John of the Cross, *The Living Flame of Love*, translated by Marjorie Flower, OCD: *The Poems of St. John of the Cross*, incorporating adaptations by Fr Iain Matthew, OCD:

> *¡Oh llama de amor viva*
> *que tiernamente hieres*
> *de mi alma en el más profundo centro!*
> *Pues ya no eres esquiva*
> *acaba ya si quieres,*
> *¡rompe la tela de este dulce encuentro!*
> *¡Oh cauterio süave!*
> *¡Oh regalada llaga!*
> *¡Oh mano blanda! ¡Oh toque delicado*
> *que a vida eterna sabe*
> *y toda deuda paga!*
> *Matando, muerte en vida has trocado.*
> *¡Oh lámparas de fuego*
> *en cuyos resplandores*
> *las profundas cavernas del sentido,*

> que estaba oscuro y ciego,
> con estraños primores
> color y luz dan junto a su querido!
> ¡Cuán manso y amoroso
> recuerdas en mi seno
> donde secretamente solo moras,
> y en tu aspirar sabroso
> de bien y gloria lleno,
> cuán delicadamente me enamoras!

2   LF: Prol. 1.
3   For more on the chronology and background of John's poems, see Tyler 2010. For both Teresa and John I will use the BAC Spanish edition of their writings and the Kavanaugh and Rodriguez translations modified where necessary. See bibliography for more details and abbreviations of texts used.
4   M: Prol. 1.
5   'Un no sé qué que quedan balbuciendo', CA: 7.
6   CA 7.9.
7   CA: 7.9.
8   LF: 4.17.
9   LF: 1:

> ¡Oh llama de amor viva,
> Que tiernamente hieres
> De mi alma en el más profundo centro!

10   LF: 1.9.
11   LF: 1.9.
12   LF: 1.10: 'Y no tiene centro de hondo y menos hondo cuantitativo.'
13   LF: 1.11.
14   LF: 1.12.
15   'Con todas sus fuerzas entienda, ame y goce a Dios.'
16   LF: 1.15.
17   LF: 1.12.
18   DN: 1.
19   CB: 1.
20   R. S. Thomas, 'Pilgrimages', in Collected Poems 1945–1990, ed. A. Motion (London: Phoenix, 2002).

21 LF: 1.12.

22 LF: 1.15.

23 LF: 1.15.

24 LF: 1.13.

25 LF: 2.8.

26 CB: 26.

27 CB: 26.4.

28 See Tyler 2010 and 2013.

29 For more on this, see Tyler 2011.

30 LF: 2.8.

31 Allison Peers uses the more provocative 'penetrate' here in his translation, while Kavanaugh uses 'reach'.

32 V: 29.13.

33 M 6.2.4.

34 See Giordano 1995 and Florencio del Niño Jesús 1924. P. Florencio's book, written before the troubles in the Holy Land in the middle of the twentieth century, gives some fascinating details about the mutual respect between the 'dervish and sufi' communities of the Holy Mountain and the Carmelite Order.

35 1 Kings 18:20–40.

36 2 Kings 2.

37 Smet 1988: 1.4.

38 Bernard Oller in the late fourteenth century wrote that 'good faith and prescription were sufficient for them' (Smet 1988: 1.18). A manuscript that comes closest to the form of the original is that preserved in the collection of Carmelite writings edited by the Catalan provincial Philip Ribot (d. 1391). Although many scholars dismiss the reliability of Ribot, Waaijman, whose account of the Rule I draw heavily on here, is happy that this manuscript gives us a close perspective on the original Rule (Waaijman 1999: 18ff.).

39 Just to complicate the scholarship, the original text of this Bull is also lost. A copy of the original is, however, still in the Vatican (see Waaijman 1999: 19).

40 France, in allegiance with the papacy, being at war with Charles V's Spanish empire.

41 Brodrick 1956: 139–42.

42 See Barthes 1971 and Munitiz and Endean 1996.

43 R: 5.6.

44 R: 8.

45 For more on these terms see my discussion in Tyler 2013.

46 'Quier sea en quanto el entendimiento es ilucidado por la virtud divina, es de más gusto y fructo spiritual que sí el que da los exercicios hubiese mucho declarado y ampliado el sentido de la historia, porque no el mucho saber harta y satisface al anima, mas el sentir y gustar de las cosas internamente.' I have used the BAC edition of the work of St Ignatius with the Ganss translation, modified as necessary. For full bibliographical details see the Bibliography.

47 See A: 2.18.

48 CB: 1, 7, 9.

49 See Tyler 2010.

50 See Nouwen 2006, Johnson 1997, Rohr 2005.

51 Johnson 1997: 4. I have made Johnson's quote gender neutral as I believe his observation carries for women as much as for men.

52 Hedermann 2007: 173.

53 CB: 1.19.

54 CB: 1.3.

55 LF: 3.28.

56 LF: 3.29.

57 A: 1.13.11.

58 LF: 3.48.

59 LF: 3. 46.

60 LF: 3.30.

61 LF: 3.30.

62 LF: 3.41.

63 LF: 3.47

64 LF: 3.46.

65 LF: 3.46.

66 LF: 3.58.

67 Chowning 2000: 3.

68 Exx: 235–6.

69 Chowning 2000: 4.
70 A: 1.6.1.
71 A: 1.6.6.
72 A: 1.11.2.
73 Griffiths 2005: 4.
74 Griffiths 2005: 6.
75 A: 1.11.5.
76 A: 1.13.11.
77 See *Anthony de Mello and the Spiritual Exercises of St Ignatius Loyola* by G. O'Collins, in *Sources of Transformation*, ed. Tyler and Howells, 2011.
78 A: 1.13.6.
79 A: 1.14.2.
80 DN: 1.

EPILOGUE

1 Johnson 1987: 144.
2 Pope Francis 2016: 21.
3 Pope Francis 2016: 23.
4 Hedermann 2007: 177.
5 Hedermann 2007: 178.
6 Kierkegaard 1956: 215.

BIBLIOGRAPHY

ABBREVIATIONS

CUP   Cambridge University Press.

DS   *Dictionnaire de Spiritualité Ascétique et Mystique Doctrine*
et Histoire, ed. M. Viller, F. Cavallera, J. de Guibert,
A. Rayez, A. Derville, P. Lamarche, A. Solignac, 1937–
present, Paris: Beauchesne.

ICS   Institute of Carmelite Studies, Washington.

ISPCK   Indian Society for Promoting Christian Knowledge.

LCL   Loeb Classical Library.

OUP   Oxford University Press.

PG   *Patrologiae Cursus Completus*, Series Graeca, ed.
J.-P. Migne, Paris, 1857–66.

PL   *Patrologiae Cursus Completus*, Series Latina, ed.
J.-P. Migne, Paris, 1844–64.

SC   *Sources Chrétiennes*, Éditions du Cerf, Paris.

SELECTED PRIMARY SOURCES

Swami Abhishiktananda (Henri Le Saux)

Diary   *Ascent to the Depth of the Heart: The Spiritual Diary*
(1948–1973) of Swami Abhishiktananda (Dom H. Le Saux),
ed. R. Panikkar, English trans. D. Fleming and J. Stuart,
New Delhi: ISPCK, 1998.

Guru   *Guru and Disciple*, New Delhi: ISPCK, 1974.

Letters   *Swami Abhishiktananda: His Life Told Through His Letters*, ed.
J. Stuart, Delhi: ISPCK, 1995.

Sacc   *Saccidānanda: A Christian Approach to Advaitic Experience*,
New Delhi: ISPCK, 1974.

Sann   *Sannyasa*, in *The Further Shore, Two Essays by Abhishiktananda*,
New Delhi: ISPCK, 1975.

Secret   *The Secret of Arunāchala: A Christian Hermit on Shiva's Holy Mountain*, Delhi: ISPCK, 1979.

St Thomas Aquinas

ST   *Summa Theologiae*, ed. T. Gilbey, London: Eyre and Spottiswoode. *Baptism and Confirmation*, trans. J. Cunningham, 1974, Vol. 57. *Penance*, trans. T. O'Brien, 1966, Vol. 60.

St Augustine of Hippo

Conf   *Confessions*, trans. J. O'Donnell, Oxford: Clarendon, 1992 (3 vols).
Augustine: Confessions, trans. F. Sheed, Indianapolis: Hackett, 2006.

Comm Gen   *On Genesis: A Refutation of the Manichees*, *Unfinished Literal Commentary on Genesis*, *The Literal Meaning of Genesis*, in *The Works of Saint Augustine: A Translation for the 21st Century*, ed. J. Rotelle, trans. E. Hill, New York: New City Press, 2002.

Hom Ps.   *Expositions of the Psalms*, in *The Works of Saint Augustine: A Translation for the 21st Century*, trans. M. Boulding, New York: New City Press, 2001–2, Part III, Vol. 15.

Ret   *The Retractions*, in *Saint Augustine: The Retractions*, in *The Fathers of the Church, a New Translation*, trans. M. Bogam, Washington: The Catholic University of America Press, 1968, Vol. 60.

Trin   *On the Trinity*, in *The Works of Saint Augustine: A Translation for the 21st Century*, ed. J. Rotelle, trans. E. Hill, New York: New City Press, 1996.

Latin texts consulted

Corpus Christianorum, Series Latina, Turnhout: Brepols, 1955–present.

Corpus Scriptorum Ecclesiasticorum Latinorum. S. Aureli Augustini, ed. J. Zycha, Prague/Vienna: F. Tempsky, 1894.

John Cassian

The Conferences, ed. B. Ramsey, New York: Newman Press, 1997.
Conférences, ed. E. Pichery, SC 42, 54, 64, Paris: Cerf, 1955–9.

Clement of Alexandria

Clément d'Alexandrie, Les Stromates, ed. A. Le Boulluec, C. Mondésert, P. Descourtieux. SC 30, 463, Paris: Cerf, 1951/2013, 2001.

St John Climacus

The Ladder of Divine Ascent, trans. C. Luibheid and N. Russell, Mahwah, NJ: Paulist Press, 1982.

Evagrius of Pontus

Evagrius Ponticus Praktikos – The Chapters on Prayer, Cistercian Studies No. 4, trans. J. Bamberger, Kalamazoo, MI: Cistercian Publications, 1981.
Sources Chrétiennes 170 and 171, *Évagre le Pontique, Traité Pratique ou Le Moine*, ed. A. Guillaumont and C. Guillaumont, Paris: Cerf, 1971.

Sigmund Freud

SE   *Standard Edition of the Complete Psychological Works of Sigmund Freud*, trans. J. Strachey, London: The Hogarth Press, including:
        Studies in Hysteria (with Josef Breuer), Vol. 2, 1893/1955.
        The Question of Lay Analysis, Vol. 20, 1926/1959.
GW   *Gesammelte Werke in Achtzehn Bänden mit einem Nachtragsband*, ed. A. Freud, E. Bibring, W. Hoffer, E. Kris and O. Isakower, Frankfurt am Main: Fischer Verlag, 1960–8.

Gottfried von Strassburg
> *Tristan*, from the text of F. Ranke, ed. R, Krohn,
> Stuttgart: Reclam, 2010 (3 vols).
> *Tristan with the 'Tristan' of Thomas*, trans. A. Hatto,
> London: Penguin, 1967.

St Ignatius of Loyola
Exx   *The Spiritual Exercises.*
R   *Reminiscences.*
> *Obras: San Ignacio de Loyola*, Madrid: Biblioteca de
> Autores Cristianos, 2014.
> *Saint Ignatius of Loyola: Personal Writings*, ed. J. Munitiz
> and P. Endean, London: Penguin, 1996.
> *The Spiritual Exercises of St Ignatius: A Literal*
> *Translation and a Contemporary Reading*, ed.
> D. Fleming, Saint Louis: The Institute of Jesuit
> Sources, 1980.

St John of the Cross
A   *The Ascent of Mount Carmel.*
DN   *The Dark Night of the Soul.*
LF   *The Living Flame of Love* – Redaction B.
CA   *The Spiritual Canticle* – Redaction A.
CB   *The Spiritual Canticle* – Redaction B.
> *San Juan de La Cruz: Obras Completas*, Madrid: Biblioteca
> de Autores Cristianos, 2002.
> *The Collected Works of St John of the Cross*, trans.
> K. Kavanaugh and O. Rodriguez, Washington: Institute
> of Carmelite Studies, 1979.

Carl Jung
CW   *The Collected Works of C.G. Jung*, trans. R. Hull and
> H. Baynes, London: Routledge, 1971/99.
> *Modern Man in Search of a Soul*, trans. W. Dell and
> H. Baynes, London: Routledge, 1933/90.

Teresa of Avila

M   *Moradas del Castillo Interior / The Interior Castle.*

V   *El Libro de La Vida / The Book of the Life.*
    Obras Completas de Santa Teresa de Jésus, ed. Efrén de la
    Madre de Dios and Otger Steggink, 9th edn, Madrid:
    Biblioteca de Autores Cristianos, 1997.
    The Collected Works of St Teresa of Avila, trans. K. Kavanaugh
    and O. Rodriguez, 3 vols. Vol. 1: 2nd edn; Vols 2 and
    3: 1st edn, Washington: Institute of Carmelite Studies,
    1980–7.

Tertullian

    On Penitence, in *Tertullian: Treatises on Penance (De
    Paenitentia)*, in *Ancient Christian Writers*, trans. W. le Saint,
    London: Longmans, Green, 1959, Vol. 28.
    Tertullien: La Pénitence, trans. C. Munier, Paris: Cerf,
    1984, SC 316.

Ludwig Wittgenstein

BEE   *Wittgenstein's Nachlass: The Bergen Electronic Edition*,
    Oxford: OUP, 2000.

BT   *The Big Typescript – TS213: German-English Scholar's
    Edition*, ed. C. Grant-Luckhardt and M. E. Aue, London:
    Wiley Blackwell, 2005.

CV   *Culture and Value*, ed. G. von Wright and H. Nyman,
    Oxford: Blackwell, 1980.

FB   *Wittgenstein Familienbriefe*, ed. B. McGuinness,
    M. Concetta Ascher, O. Pfersmann, Frankfurt: Hölder-
    Pichler-Tempsky, 1996.

GT   *Geheime Tagebücher 1914–1916*, ed. W Baum, Vienna:
    Turia and Kant, 1992.

LC   *Lectures and Conversations on Aesthetics, Psychology and
    Religious Belief*, ed. C. Barrett, Oxford: Blackwell, 1989.

LF   *Letters to Ludwig von Ficker,* in 'Wittgenstein: Sources and
    Perspectives', ed. C. G. Luckhardt, London: Harvester,
    1979.

LPE   *Letters from Ludwig Wittgenstein with a Memoir by Paul Engelmann*, ed. B. McGuinness, Oxford: Blackwell, 1967.

LR   *Letters to Russell, Keynes and Moore*, ed. G. H. von Wright, Oxford: Blackwell, 1974.

NB   *Notebooks 1914–1916*, trans. G. E. M. Anscombe, Oxford: Blackwell, 1984.

PI   *Philosophical Investigations*, ed. G. E. M. Anscombe and R. Rhees, Oxford: Blackwell, 1958.

PO   *Philosophical Occasions 1912–1951*, ed. J. Klagge and A. Nordmann, Cambridge: Hackett, 1993.

PPO   *Public and Private Occasions*, ed. J. Klagge and A. Nordmann, New York: Rowman and Littlefield, 2003.

PU   *Philosophische Untersuchungen*, in *Werkausgabe in 8 Bände*, Vol. 1, Frankfurt am Main: Suhrkamp, 1993.

RFGB   *Remarks on Frazer's Golden Bough*, reprinted in *Philosophical Occasions 1912–1951*, ed. J. C. Klagge and A. Nordmann, Cambridge: Hackett, 1993.

T   *Tractatus Logico-Philosophicus*, trans. D. F. Pears and B. McGuinness, London: Routledge & Kegan Paul, 1961.

VB   *Vermischte Bemerkungen*, in Volume 8: *Werkausgabe in 8 Bände*, Frankfurt am Main: Suhrkamp, 1993.

W   *Werkausgabe in 8 Bände*, Frankfurt am Main: Suhrkamp, 1993.

Z   *Zettel*, ed. G. E. M. Anscombe and G. H. von Wright, Oxford: Blackwell, 1967.

Church Documents and Scripture

Decrees of the Ecumenical Councils, ed. N. Tanner. Cambridge: CUP, 1990.

Les Conciles Oecuméniques De Nicée à Latran V., Vol. 2 *Les Décrets*, ed. G. Alberigo, Paris: Les Éditions du Cerf, 1994.

Hindu Scriptures, trans. R. C. Zaehner, London: Dent, 1966.

The Complete Dead Sea Scrolls in English, ed. G. Vermes, London: Allen Lane, 1997.

The Documents of Vatican II, ed. W. Abbott, London: Geoffrey Chapman, 1966.

Scripture Quotations from the *New Revised Standard Version*,
London: Harper, 2007, with modifications as necessary.

Other Works
St Athanasius (1998), *The Life of St Anthony*, trans. C. White,
London: Penguin.
Barthes, R. (1971), *Sade, Fourier, Loyola*, Paris: Éditions du Seuil.
Bédier, M. (1913), *The Romance of Tristan and Iseult Drawn from
the Best French Sources and Retold by J. Bédier*, trans. H. Belloc,
London: George Allen.
Berggren, E. (1975), *The Psychology of Confession*, Leiden: Brill.
Brodrick, J. (1956), *Saint Ignatius Loyola: The Pilgrim Years 1491–
1538*, San Francisco: Ignatius Press.
Cavell, S. (1976), *Must We Mean What We Say? A Book of Essays*, New
York: Charles Scribner's Sons.
Cavell, S. (1979), *The Claim of Reason: Wittgenstein, Skepticism,
Morality and Tragedy*, Oxford and New York: OUP.
Chowning, D. (2000), 'Free to Love: Negation in the Doctrine
of John of the Cross', in *Carmelite Studies* 6, Washington:
ICS.
Chryssavgis, J. (2003), *In the Heart of the Desert: The Spirituality of
the Desert Fathers and Mothers*, Bloomington, IN: World Wisdom
Press.
Cornwell, J. (2014), *The Dark Box: A Secret History of Confession*,
London: Profile.
Crary, A. and Read, R. (2000), *The New Wittgenstein*, London:
Routledge.
Dallen, J. (1991), *The Reconciling Community: The Rite of Penance*,
Collegeville, MN: The Liturgical Press.
D'Costa, G. (1990), ed. *Christian Uniqueness Reconsidered*,
Maryknoll, NY: Orbis.
De Rougemont, D. (1963), *The Myths of Love*, trans. R. Howard,
London: Faber and Faber.
De Rougemont, D. (1983), *Love in the Western World*, trans. M.
Belgion, Princeton, NJ: Princeton University Press.
Du Boulay, S. (2005), *The Cave of the Heart: The Life of Swami
Abhishiktananda*, Maryknoll, NY: Orbis.

Engelmann, P. (1967), *Letters from Ludwig Wittgenstein with a Memoir*, Oxford: Blackwell.

Florencio del Niño Jesús (1924), *El Monte Carmelo: Tradiciones e Historia de La Santa Montaña, de la Virgen del Carmen y De La Orden Carmelitana y la Luz do Los Monumentos y Documentos*, Madrid: Mensajero de Santa Teresa.

Foucault, M. (1998), *The History of Sexuality: Volume One, The Will to Knowledge*, trans. R. Hurley, London: Penguin.

Foucault, M. (1998), *The History of Sexuality: Volume Two, The Use of Pleasure*, trans. R. Hurley, London: Penguin.

Friesen, J. (2001), *Abhishiktānanda's Non-Monistic Advaitic Experience*, PhD thesis, University of South Africa.

Giordano, S. (1995), *Carmel in the Holy Land: From Its Beginnings to the Present Day*, Arenzano: Il Messaggero di Gesu Bambino.

Griffiths, B. (2005), 'Letter to Dr Mary Allen', reprinted in *The Bede Griffiths Sangha Newsletter*, March 2005, Vol. 8: 1.

Hedermann, M. P. (2007), *Symbolism: The Glory of Escutcheoned Doors*, Dublin: Veritas.

Hosseini, M. (2007), *Wittgenstein und Weisheit*, Stuttgart: Kohlhammer.

Johannessen, K., Larsen, R. and Åmås, K. (1994), *Wittgenstein and Norway*, Oslo: Solum Forlag.

Johnson, R. (1987), *The Psychology of Romantic Love*, London: Penguin.

Johnson, R. (1996), *Balancing Heaven and Earth: A Memoir*, New York: HarperCollins.

Johnson, R. (1997), *He: Understanding Masculine Psychology*, New York: Harper.

Kerr, F. (1997), *Theology after Wittgenstein*, Oxford: Blackwell.

Kierkegaard, S. (1956), *Purity of Heart is to Will One Thing: Spiritual Preparation for the Office of Confession*, trans. D. Steere, New York: Harper.

Kittel, G. (1967), *Theological Dictionary of the New Testament*, trans. G. Bromiley, Grand Rapids, MI: Eerdmans.

Klagge, J. (2001), *Wittgenstein: Biography and Philosophy*, Cambridge: CUP.

Malcolm, N. (2001), *Ludwig Wittgenstein: A Memoir*, Oxford: Clarendon.

Marion, J.-L. (2005), '*Mihi magna quaestio factus sum*: The Privilege of Unknowing', in *Journal of Religion* 85 (2005): 1–24.

Marion, J.-L. (2012), *In the Self's Place: The Approach of Saint Augustine*, Stanford, CA: Stanford University Press.

Martin, N. (2005), 'North Indian Hindi Devotional Literature', in *The Blackwell Companion to Hinduism*, Oxford: Blackwell.

McGinn, B. (1991), *The Presence of God: A History of Western Christian Mysticism – Vol. I: The Foundations of Mysticism*, London: SCM.

McGinn, B. (2010), 'Humans as *Imago Dei*: Mystical Anthropology Then and Now', in *Sources of Transformation: Revitalising Christian Spirituality*, ed. P. M. Tyler and E. Howells, London: Continuum.

McGinn, B. (2016), *True Confessions: Augustine and Teresa of Avila on the Mystical Self*, in *Teresa of Avila: Mystical Theology and Spirituality in the Carmelite Tradition*, ed. P. M. Tyler and E. Howells, London: Routledge.

McGuinness, B. (1988), *Wittgenstein: A Life – The Young Ludwig (1889–1921)*, London: Penguin.

Monk, R. (1990), *Ludwig Wittgenstein: The Duty of Genius*, London: Jonathan Cape.

Nandhikkara, J. (2011), *Being Human After Wittgenstein: A Philosophical Anthropology*, Vol. 1, Bangalore: Dharmaram.

Nouwen, H. (2006), *The Wounded Healer: Ministry in Contemporary Society*, London: Darton, Longman and Todd.

O'Collins, G. (2011), *Anthony de Mello and the Spiritual Exercises of St Ignatius Loyola*, in *Sources of Transformation*, ed. P. M. Tyler and E. Howells, London: Continuum.

Panikkar, R. (1973), *The Trinity and the Religious Experience of Man*, New York: Orbis.

Panikkar, R. (2014), *Mysticism and Spirituality*, Vol. 1, Part 2: *Spirituality: The Way of Life*, in *Opera Omnia*, ed. M. Carrara Pavan, Maryknoll, NY: Orbis.

Perumpallikunnel, K. (2009), 'Mystical Experience: Fount and Raison D'être of *Sannyāsa*', in *New Horizons of Indian Christian Living*, ed. S. Chackalackal, Bengaluru: Vidyavanam.

Pope Francis (2015), *Laudato Si', On Care for Our Common Home*, London: Catholic Truth Society.

Pope Francis (2016), *The Name of God is Mercy*, trans. O. Stransky, London: Bluebird.

Rahner, K. (1969), *Sacramentum Mundi: An Encyclopedia of Theology*, ed. with C. Ernst and K. Smyth, London: Burns and Oates.

Rahner, K. (1983), *Theological Investigations*, Vol. XV, *Penance in the Early Church*, trans. L. Swain, London: Darton, Longman and Todd.

Rhees, R. (1987), *Recollections of Wittgenstein*, Oxford: Oxford Paperback.

Rohr, R. (2005), *From Wild Man to Wise Man: Reflections on Male Spirituality*, New York: St Anthony Messenger Press.

Rohr, R. and Martos, J. (1996), *The Wild Man's Journey: Reflections on Male Spirituality*, Cincinnati, Ohio: St Anthony Messenger Press.

Smet, J. (1988), *The Carmelites: A History of The Brothers of Our Lady of Mount Carmel* (3 vols), Illinois: Carmelite Spiritual Center.

Smith, C. (2004), *The Way of Paradox: Spiritual Life as Taught by Meister Eckhart*, London: Darton, Longman and Todd.

Sontag, F. (2000), *Wittgenstein and the Mystical: Philosophy as an Ascetic Practice*, Atlanta, Georgia: Scholars Press.

Tagore, R. (1961), *Towards Universal Man*, Bombay: Asia Publishing House.

Tagore, R. (1996), 'The Fourfold Way of India', reprinted in *The English Writings of Rabindranath Tagore*, Vol III, ed. S. Kumar Das, New Delhi: Sahitya Akademi.

Taylor, C. (2010), *The Culture of Confession from Augustine to Foucault: A Genealogy of the 'Confessing Animal'*, London: Routledge.

Thomas, R. S. (2002), *Collected Poems 1945–1990*, ed. A. Motion, London: Phoenix.

Thottakara, A. (2009), '*Sannyāsa*: Dynamics of a Life of Renunciation', in *New Horizons of Indian Christian Living*, ed. S. Chackalackal, Bengaluru: Vidyavanam.

Tolstoy, L. (1895), *The Four Gospels*, Croydon: The Brotherhood Publishing Company.

Tolstoy, L. (1904), *My Confession: Critique of Dogmatic Theology*, in *The Complete Works of Count Tolstoy*, Vol. 13 (1879–1882), trans. L. Wiener, London: Dent and Co.

Tranströmer, T. (2011), *New Collected Poems*, trans. R. Fulton, Highgreen, Northumberland: Bloodaxe.

Trapè, A. (1986), 'VI. Saint Augustine', in *Patrology*, Vol. 4, *The Golden Age of Latin Patristic Literature from the Council of Nicea to the Council of Chalcedon*, ed. A. Di Berardino, Westminster: Christian Classics.

Tyler, P. M. (2010), *St John of the Cross: Outstanding Christian Thinker*, London: Continuum.

Tyler, P. M. (2011), *The Return to the Mystical: Ludwig Wittgenstein, Teresa of Avila and the Western Mystical Tradition*, London: Continuum.

Tyler, P. M. (2013), 'The Psychology of Vocation: Nurturing the Grail Quest', in *The Disciple's Call: Theologies of Vocation from Scripture to the Present Day*, ed. C. Jamison, London: Bloomsbury.

Tyler, P. M. (2013a), *Teresa of Avila: Doctor of the Soul*, London: Bloomsbury.

Tyler, P. M. (2016), *The Pursuit of the Soul: Psychoanalysis, Soul-making and the Christian Tradition*, Edinburgh: T&T Clark.

Tyler, P. M. and Howells, E., eds (2016a), *Teresa of Avila: Mystical Theology and Contemplation in the Carmelite Tradition*, London: Routledge.

Vineeth, F. (2004), *The Asian Vision of God*, Bangalore: Vidyavanam.

Waaijman, K. (1999), *The Mystical Space of Carmel: A Commentary on the Carmelite Rule*, Leuven: Peeters.

Ward, B., ed. (1984), *The Sayings of the Desert Fathers: The Alphabetical Collection*, Kalamazoo, MI: Cistercian Publications.

Ware, K. (1982), *Introduction* to *The Ladder of Divine Ascent*, trans. C. Luibheid and N. Russell, Mahwah, NJ: Paulist Press.

Williams, R. (1990), *Trinity and Pluralism*, in *Christian Uniqueness Reconsidered*, ed. G. D'Costa, Maryknoll, NY: Orbis.

INDEX

A NOTE ON THE AUTHOR

Peter Tyler is Professor of Pastoral Theology and Spirituality and Director of the Centre for Initiatives in Spirituality and Reconciliation (InSpiRe) at St Mary's University, Twickenham, London. For the past three decades he has pursued the reconciliation of psychotherapy and spirituality through writings, counselling therapy, retreats and public lectures. His most recent book, the beginning of a proposed trilogy, is *The Pursuit of the Soul: Psychoanalysis, Soul-making and the Christian Tradition* (Bloomsbury, T & T Clark, 2016).

A NOTE ON THE TYPE

The text of this book is set in Perpetua. This typeface is an adaptation of a style of letter that had been popularised for monumental work in stone by Eric Gill. Large scale drawings by Gill were given to Charles Malin, a Parisian punch-cutter, and his hand-cut punches were the basis for the font issued by Monotype. First used in a private translation called 'The Passion of Perpetua and Felicity', the italic was originally called Felicity.